D0030231

Interpreting Difficult Texts

INTERPRETING DIFFICULT TEXTS

Anti-Judaism and Christian Preaching

CLARK M. WILLIAMSON
AND
RONALD J. ALLEN

SCM PRESS
London

TRINITY PRESS INTERNATIONAL
Philadelphia

First published 1989

SCM Press
26–30 Tottenham Road
London N1 4BZ

Trinity Press International
3725 Chestnut Street
Philadelphia, Pa. 19104

All rights reserved. No part of this publication may be
reproduced, stored in a retrieval system, or transmitted,
in any form or by any means, electronic, mechanical,
photocopying, recording or otherwise, without the prior
permission of the publishers, SCM Press and Trinity
Press International.

Copyright © Clark M. Williamson and Ronald J. Allen 1989

British Library Cataloguing in Publication Data

Williamson, Clark M.
  Interpreting difficult texts: anti-Judaism and
  Christian preaching.
  1. Bible. N. T. Special subjects: Judaism
  I. Title   II. Allen, Ronald J.
  296

  ISBN 0–334–02062–X

Library of Congress Cataloging-in-Publication Data

Williamson, Clark M.
  Interpreting difficult texts.

  Bibliography: p.
  1. Judaism—Controversial literature—History and
criticism.   2. Bible. N. T.—Homiletical use.
3. Christianity and antisemitism.   4. Judaism
(Christian theology)   I. Allen, Ronald J.
(Ronald James), 1949–   .   II. Title.
BM585.W5 1989   261.2'6   89–4554
ISBN 0–334–02062–X

Photoset by Input Typesetting Ltd
and printed in Great Britain by
Richard Clay Ltd, Bungay, Suffolk

Contents

Preface

One of the most significant movements in contemporary Christian scholarship and theological reflection is the one which sees, in the words of Johann-Baptist Metz, that "Christian theology does not know whereof it speaks" unless it recognizes that it speaks "after Auschwitz". Although still a comparatively small movement, nonetheless it has already produced shelves of books in the areas of biblical studies, historical theology, dogmatic theology and ethics, all seeking to clarify the reality of anti-Judaism in Christian history. As a result, a growing number of Christian clergy are aware of the "teaching of contempt" and properly reject it.

What does not exist, so far, is a book that tries to offer practical help to preachers, help that enables them to confront the anti-Judaism found in texts from scripture and, sometimes in spite of the text, to preach the gospel. This book was written to provide precisely such help. Its intended audience includes practicising parish pastors and students of homiletics who seek assistance in implementing in practice what they have learned of the history and practice of Christian anti-Judaism.

This book was written by two authors, one a scholar of the Bible and homiletics, and the other a systematic theologian, a combination not often found together. The former, Ron Allen, wrote Chapters 3, 5 and 7; the latter, Clark Williamson, wrote Chapters 1, 2 and 4. Each of us contributed sermons to Chapter 6. Each chapter was revised by its author in the light of the other author's criticism.

The authors express their appreciation to Joy Sherrill, who typed about half the final manuscript from a rough draft. The book is dedicated to all hard-working preachers who strive to teach the Christian faith in ways that are appropriate to the gospel, credible, and morally plausible.

Ronald J. Allen
Clark M. Williamson

— 1 —

Anti-Judaism: What It Is and Why It Should Go

Introduction

In this book we contend that anti-Judaism sometimes shows up in the preaching of the church, that it ought not to appear there, and that it can be avoided by careful attention to preaching the gospel instead of an ideology. The purpose of this chapter is to define anti-Judaism and to offer a set of reasons as to why it is inappropriate in Christian preaching, the purpose of which it obstructs.

We do not hold that anti-Judaism is always present in Christian preaching, nor that it is inherently or necessarily there. If we did, there would be no point in writing this book. But we do maintain that anti-Judaism rears its ugly head far too often in the church's preaching and that its continuing presence, this long after Auschwitz, is intolerable.

What is Christian anti-Judaism?

The reasons which we will give for excising anti-Judaism from Christian preaching become more convincing the greater our acquaintance with anti-Judaism. Anti-Judaism is one way (fortunately there are others) of interpreting, explaining or setting forth the Christian faith. It is most easily grasped if we see it as turning upon six themes (we do not claim that these themes exhaustively describe anti-Judaism, but that they indicate it).

1. Jews and Judaism serve as the images of everything bad in religion

The role of Jews and Judaism as portraying everything bad that can occur in religion is one that preachers are easily tempted to draw. Years ago a preacher described what a Christian congregation should be like. In the process he characterized what it should *not* be like by drawing a picture of four negative kinds of congregations. These were the excessively establishmentarian congregation, unwilling to change; the excessively revolutionary congregation, too ready to challenge everybody and everything; the extraordinarily withdrawn congregation, hiding from the world; and the compromised congregation that stood midway between withdrawal and establishment.

All these were contrasted with the genuinely Christian and authentically prophetic church. The problem with this otherwise good sermon was that each of the "bad" kinds of congregations was given a Jewish name. The established congregation was Sadducean, the revolutionary congregation was composed of Zealots, the withdrawn one was Essene, and the compromisers were Pharisees.

There are many other ways in which Jews and Judaism are used to portray everything bad in religion. They are said to believe in works-righteousness instead of grace, the letter instead of the spirit, legalism instead of radical obedience, commitment to an old, dead past rather than openness to God's new future, and so forth. Every faith has adherents who fail to get the point, and just as there are Christians no doubt there are Jews who are legalistic, works-righteous and all the rest. What we Christians have done for a long time, however, is to criticize as "Jewish" everything that goes wrong in Christianity. Thereby we give the impression that Judaism is necessarily bad and that Jews can never be otherwise, while Christianity is inherently all the good things that Judaism can never be. Using Jews and Judaism as negative images of the worst things in religion is probably the most popular form of anti-Judaism in Christian preaching today. To avoid it, preachers should use Christian names for Christian sins and practice prophetic *self*-criticism.

2. The cleavage between promise and denunciation

In the history of the church's preaching and teaching *adversus Judaeos* (against the Jews), a sharp break is made between the two poles of prophetic thought. "The dialectical structure of prophetic thought was split apart, so that its affirmative side, of forgiveness and promise, was assigned to the Christian church, while its negative side, of divine wrath and rejection, was read out against the Jews" (Ruether, 1983: 34). Obviously this strategy fits nicely with regarding Jews and Judaism as representing everything bad in religion. This division between promise and criticism projects an unremitting parody of evil upon the Jewish people, a people with whom Christians no longer regard themselves as identified.

When this theme is articulated, the church regards itself as in principle above prophetic self-criticism; it "stands triumphant and perfect" (Ruether, 1983: 34). Hebraic and Jewish capacity for internal self-criticism is turned into an external and relentless condemnation. It is possible that the historical Jesus engaged in criticism of inauthentic religion, but such activity would clearly stand in the tradition of Jewish faith. The shift from internal prophetic criticism to anti-Judaism came when the later church no longer criticized hypocritical ways of living the Law and, instead, condemned the Law (Torah, path, instruction) as necessarily hypocritical. To avoid falling into this theme, preachers need to remember that the genuine prophet always identifies with the people being criticized and that Jewish faith, whether of Jesus' day or now, possesses the same religious vitality and integrity as Christian faith.

3. The rupture between universalism and particularism

Christian anti-Judaism also comes to expression in the claim that the church, sometimes called the "new Israel" (a name which does not occur in the scriptures), is a universal community in contrast to the old, particularist and ethnocentric Jews. Thus in the very name of universalism, a new kind of exclusivism and antagonism is created. Such a universalism is barely distinguishable from a triumphalism towards all other peoples, but particularly towards Jews who are now looked upon as beyond salvation (unless they cease being Jews by becoming Christians). A genuine Christian universalism must affirm the pluralism of human beings and of diverse historical ways of experiencing ultimacy and mediating that experience to others. What is universal about Christian faith is that it points beyond itself to the One who is universal. Preachers can avoid making idolatrous claims on behalf of Christianity or the church by remembering that God transcends the church and that no historical, relative faith, however important, is final, ultimate, or universal.

4. The breach between old and new Adam, letter and spirit, law and grace

As the church became increasingly, and then exclusively, Gentile and decreasingly Jewish, it saw itself as displacing Judaism. Judaism was viewed as old, as letter, and as law, whereas the church was new, spiritual and grace-filled. Judaism was fleshliness and carnality, Israel of the flesh, and Christianity was the new Israel of the spirit. The theological error involved here, as Rosemary Ruether well states it, is that "the distinction between ambiguous historical existence and perfected messianic life is imported into history to define the line between two peoples and two historical eras" (Ruether, 1983: 40). The result is to mystify the reality of Christian life, to talk and think as though Christianity were devoid of flesh, law, and letter. Yet every faith, Christianity included, is embodied in letter, law and flesh; indeed, Christianity has multiplied so many fleshly embodiments of itself that their very number and dividedness long ago became an ecumenical scandal. The spirit of faith is necessarily embodied in institutions, texts, creeds, councils, liturgies, etc. Preachers can avoid indulging in these dichotomies by remembering the theological truth that perfection is ahead of the church which lives in response to God's calling of it forward. A full generation after the resurrection Paul the apostle declared: "I consider that the sufferings of this present time are not worth comparing with the glory that is to be revealed to us" (Romans 8.18). Christianity lives from a gospel of promise that calls us to hope in a fulfilment not yet seen. Christians and Jews look forward to the same future and live out of the same dialectic between foretaste and hope.

5. The Jews were rejected because of their crimes

The claim made by anti-Judaism is that the church displaces the Jewish people in covenant with God; that when the church was elected the Jews were rejected. The chief reason given for their abandonment is that they had killed Christ, indeed, that their whole history was a "trail of crime". As they killed Jesus, so they killed the prophets. This theme reaches back into the Gospels and Acts (Luke 11.47; Acts 2.23; 3.15; 5.30), but the fathers of the church embroider it considerably, accusing Jews of every conceivable kind of crime, including idolatry, law-breaking, vice and prostitution. Israel becomes the harlot people who in their blasphemy, rebelliousness, gluttony and sensuality would not flinch at killing the Son of God.

Readers unfamiliar with the catalogue of Christian slander against Jews will doubtless recoil from this list, saying "surely not!" In the following description of Christian preaching against the Jews, we will provide examples. With regard to the basic claim of this theme, that "the Jews" killed Christ (which is about as intelligible as saying that "the Americans" killed Martin Luther King, Jr), we need little convincing. We have all heard sermons, particularly around Palm Sunday and Good Friday, in which this hoary allegation was fervently repeated.

How can preachers avoid repeating this slander, particularly when dealing with texts in which it appears? Chiefly by remembering that they are commissioned to preach the gospel, which does not lie.

6. Anti-Judaism is an interpretative model for "understanding" Christianity and Judaism

In a creative suggestion, David P. Efroymson proposes that we look upon anti-Judaism as a model: both a model *of* and a model *for*. First, it is a model *of* Judaism, according to which Judaism is a system and Jews a people "rejected by God, unfaithful to God, rejecting Christ, opposed to Christianity, and caught up in the crimes appropriate to their carnality, hardness, blindness and *vetustas* [obdurate commitment to what is past and gone, oldness]" (Efroymson, 1976: 223). Whereas Jews are a people of the past, disobedience and sterility, Christians are "a people and a system of newness, of fidelity, of spirituality, of moral vigor, and of universality" (Efroymson, 1976: 224). Anti-Judaism is also a model *for*, as Efroymson says:

> A model for action, for acting "ethically", for praying or worshiping "spiritually", for reading the Bible accurately – all in specific and clearly focused distinction from the Jewish way of acting, praying, and of reading the Bible (Efroymson, 1976: 224).

This interpretative scheme, which really is not a sixth point so much as a summary of the first five and an indication of how they constitute a perspective, will appear in the survey of anti-Judaism in Christian preaching, to which we will turn in the second chapter. Our immediate task is to provide reasons why the whole approach to reading, interpreting and preaching on biblical texts is inappropriate to the Christian message and should not be heard from Christian pulpits.

Out of character with the gospel

What is Christian preaching and why is anti-Judaism inappropriate to it? When we preach, we are teaching the Christian faith, making the Christian witness and telling the Christian story. As we do this, we need to see to it that the witness which we bear or the story which we tell is appropriate to the Christian tradition, that it makes sense, and that it is moral. We need to ask ourselves whether we are preaching the gospel of Jesus Christ or an ideology; whether it is the Word of God or some other word that we are setting forth; whether we have the story straight.

The first reason why it is imperative to eliminate anti-Judaism from Christian preaching is that anti-Judaism contradicts the good news which it is the preacher's task to re-present to the congregation. That good news is about the radical grace of God,

God's unbounded love, the wideness of God's mercy that is extended freely to absolutely everybody, *even* us. Anti-Judaism is an exclusivism, an us-them, insider-outsider point of view, that makes being one of us the condition for gaining access to God's love and grace. It is a works-righteousness, with all the demonstrated deadliness in Christian history that works-righteousness always brings in its wake.

The second reason for banishing anti-Judaism from preaching is that is simply incredible. It works with a view of God that imagines God (by the way, patriarchally) as a finite being (an in-the-world being) who cuts deals with individuals and groups, adopting some from disfavour into favour and dismissing others from favour into disfavour. It depends on a view of God as making and breaking covenants in the way that ambitious and unscrupulous people make and break contracts. This wheeler-dealer, little "g" god is nothing more than the figment of a limited imagination. The only view of God that is both credible and appropriate to the biblical witness is of a God who is unfailingly faithful and unfailingly related and gracious to each and all, not an in-the-world being but the One in whom the world finds its being.

The third reason for eradicating anti-Judaism from Christian preaching is that it is immoral. Anti-Judaism is doubly immoral, having immoral consequences for both Christians and Jews. For Jews the record is clear. The anti-Judaism of Christian preaching was incorporated in the social fabric of Christendom, in ecclesial and secular legislation against Jews, in political and economic disenfranchisement, in popular prejudice, in ridiculous charges of child murder, host desecration and well-poisoning, and in pogroms that steadily increased in intensity (Ruether, 1974: 183–225; Williamson, 1982: 106–22). Nor can such murderous consequences be dismissed as "medieval", not when the worst of them occurred within living memory.

While the United States has always been different from Europe because the link between throne and altar was broken by the first amendment to the Constitution, that does not mean that Christianity in America is free from responsibility for anti-Judaism and its results. A major study of antisemitism in

America concludes that "Christianity continues to have a strong impact upon what people think about Jews" and that it is "second only to a lack of education as a primary source of anti-Semitic prejudice among Americans" (Quinley and Glock: 109). That prejudice against contemporary Jews is learned and reinforced in church is shown by another study: the clergy are as likely as the laity "to blame Jews both historically and down through the generations to modern times for the death of Jesus". Concluding that too many clergy are "wayward shepherds", these sociologists comment that "when both sheep and shepherds are wayward in the same direction and to the same degree, it seems unrealistic to blame only the sheep" (Stark *et al.*: 57). In spite of official church pronouncements to the contrary, about one-third of the clergy still blame "the Jews" for crucifying Christ (Stark *et al.*: 41). The evidence is clear that their parishioners believe what they hear and as a result harbour negative attitudes towards their Jewish neighbours.

The negative moral consequence for Christians has been the tendency to be insufferably smug, to regard one's religion and oneself as superior and others as inferior, an attitude hardly conducive to the command of the gospel that we are to love our neighbours as ourselves. In relation to the neighbour and the neighbour's needs, said Luther, each of us is to be "a perfectly dutiful servant of all, subject to all" (Luther, 1961: 53). The self-satisfied bovine complacency that comes from being aware of one's superiority to others is incompatible with the life of grace which Christians are given and called to lead.

— 2 —

Anti-Judaism in Christian Preaching

Introduction

Having looked at a definition of anti-Judaism and offered a set of reasons why it should be eliminated from Christian preaching, we now turn to a survey of preaching from the first century to the present. Our purpose in doing this is to show that what we are talking about is a real and persistent problem, and that the presence of anti-Judaism in preaching is bought at the price of the absence of the gospel.

Early and patristic preaching

As the early church became composed of Hellenistic Jews committed to the Christian mission to Gentiles, it increasingly distanced itself from Jews and the Judaisms of its day. Its preaching more and more took on an accusatorial tone against Jews. C. H. Dodd used to contend that the four sermons of Peter in Acts 2–4 "represent not what Peter said upon this or that occasion, but the *kerygma* of the Church at Jerusalem at an early period" (Dodd: 21). Most Lucan scholars today think that the sermons represent the message of a later Christian community. At least from the time of Luke, this history is riddled with anti-Judaism. According to Acts, a text of the Hellenistic Jewish Christian mission, Peter says to the "men of Israel" that "this Jesus, . . . you crucified and killed by the hands of lawless men" (Acts 2.23). The first sermon ends: "Let all the house of Israel therefore know assuredly that God has

made him both Lord and Christ, this Jesus whom you crucified"
(Acts 2.36).

The claim that Peter's contemporary hearers had killed
Christ surfaces again in the third sermon: "The God of Abraham
and of Isaac and of Jacob, the God of our fathers, glorified his
servant Jesus, whom you delivered up and denied in the
presence of Pilate, when he had decided to release him. But you
denied the Holy and Righteous One, and asked for a murderer
to be granted to you, and killed the Author of life, whom God
raised from the dead. To this we are witnesses" (Acts 3.13–15).
Peter repeats the refrain in his fourth sermon to the "rulers of
the people and elders", referring to "the name of Jesus Christ
of Nazareth, whom you crucified . . ." (Acts 4.10). In these
sermons the church "confesses" the sins of the Jews, not its
own. The accusation *tua culpa*, you are guilty, is not the
confession *mea culpa*, I am guilty.

How the preaching of the church became accusatorial against
the Jews had much to do with conflict between the synagogue
and the church in the late first century and persecutions
brought upon the small and struggling Christian communities
(Stambaugh and Balch: 60ff.). Yet the later charge of deicide
has its roots in the claim that the Jews "killed the Author of
life", and it is kept alive by an uncritical reading of texts shaped
in an era of conflict. In the patristic era, anti-Judaism as an
interpretative scheme and its five themes regularly appear in
Christian preaching. What follows, far from being an exhaustive
account, barely hints at its scope and depth.

1. Melito of Sardis

Melito, who died about 190, was Bishop of Sardis, capital of
Lydia in west Asia Minor. His sermon, *On the Passover*, was
discovered in this century and published in 1940. In it he treats
the "Old Testament" as containing "parables" and "types" of
the New and compares them with an architect's model which
exhibits the shape of what is to be but is replaced by the real
thing. Hence Israel is replaced by the church, the law by the
gospel, the paschal lamb by Christ. Melito was also a modalist,
regarding Christ as God in a "mode", so he can talk of the

crucifixion as killing God: "God is murdered." Here is his sketch/reality hermeneutic at work:

> The people then was a model by way of preliminary sketch,
> and the law was the writing of a parable;
> the gospel is the recounting and fulfilment of the law,
> and the church is the repository of the reality.
> The model then was precious before the reality,
> and the parable was marvellous before the interpretation;
> that is, the people were precious before the church arose,
> and the law was marvellous before the gospel was elucidated.
> But when the church arose
> and the gospel took precedence,
> the model was made void, conceding its power to the reality,
> and the law was fulfilled, conceding its power to the gospel
> (Melito: 21).

To this way of understanding Christianity as the fulfilment and emptying of Judaism, which is now void, Melito adds the charge of deicide: "He who hung the earth is hanging; he who fixed the heavens has been fixed; he who fastened the universe has been fastened to a tree; the Sovereign has been insulted; the God has been murdered; the King of Israel has been put to death by an Israelite right hand" (Melito: 55). As a result, says Melito to Israel, "you lie dead, but he has risen from the dead" (Melito: 57). Melito's sermon is one of the earliest Christian sermons that we have, and one of the most elegant. It warns us that Christian preaching, however elegant, can proclaim terrible things.

2. Proclus

In a sermon on the occasion of the festival of the Virgin Mary, Proclus, patriarch of Constantinople, discoursed (*c*. 431) on the doctrines of Mary as the Mother of God and on the divine-human person of Christ. He assures his hearers of the truth of his views "even if the Jews disbelieve the Lord who has said so", i.e., that Christ was the word incarnate (Proclus: 63). "So he who bought [redeemed] us was no mere man, you Jew" (Proclus: 65)! Understandably (for Proclus) the church was outraged when she saw the synagogue crowning him with thorns (Proclus: 66)

3. Augustine

Augustine, Bishop of Hippo in northern Africa from *c.* 396– *c.* 430, in a sermon on sin and grace, works the law/grace dichotomy. He urges his hearers not to believe that "the law is enough for us", arguing: "What the law produced was fear" (Augustine, 1975: 125). What was received at Sinai "was the spirit of slavery". The Jews know as their founding event only "the shadow of the Passover", but at the beginnings of the church the holy spirit "actually settled", on the apostles: "This time it was not with fear but with love, so that we might be sons and not slaves" (Augustine, 1975: 125). The fear/love, law/grace dichotomy leads to the old/new schism: "This is the New Testament, not the Old. 'Old things have passed away, behold all things are become new. And all this is from God' " [II Cor. 5.17–18] (Augustine, 1975: 126).

Explaining the petition in the Lord's Prayer "Thy will be done on earth as it is in heaven", Augustine proclaims: "O Church of God, thy enemy is the heathen, the Jew, the heretic; he is the earth" (Augustine, 1971: 133). Augustine continues by urging his listeners to pray for their enemies, but what is intriguing is his identification of Jews as Jews with the enemies of the church. They are an alien other, over against whom the church works out its identity.

4. Cyril of Jerusalem

About the year 350, Cyril of Jerusalem, in a lecture to about-to-be-baptized students of the Christian faith, articulated the doctrine of the "one holy catholic church". In his discussion, he distinguished between the "first assembly" of the Jews and the "second assembly" of the church: "But since then the Jews have fallen out of favour because of their conspiring against the Lord, and the Saviour has built up from among the Gentiles a second assembly or Church . . ." (Cyril of Jerusalem, 1975a: 167). He interprets Psalm 26.5, "I have hated the church of the evil doers", as a prophecy that the Jews would be cast off, and

Psalm 26.8, "Lord, I have loved the beauty of thine house", as a prophecy "of the second church that is abuilding". Since the church that was in Judaea was cast off, he avers, "henceforth the churches of Christ abound in all the world". Applying denunciation to Jews and promises to Christians, he interprets "I have no pleasure in you" as God's rejection of the Jews and applies to the church the statement, "from the rising of the sun even unto the going down of the same, my name shall be great among the Gentiles" [Mal. 1.10–11]. He concludes: "For after the rejection of the first church, then (as Paul says) in the second and Catholic Church, 'God has set first apostles, second prophets, third teachers, after that miracles, then gifts of healings, helps, governments, diversities of tongues'; yes, and every sort of virtue . . ." (Cyril of Jerusalem, 1975a: 168). The new, catholic, Gentile church displaces the old particularistic Jews in God's favour.

The sacraments receive a similar interpretation from Cyril. The bread and wine of the eucharist are not to be thought of in the same light as the use of bread and wine in Judaism: "in the old covenant there was the shewbread. But that, since it belonged to the old covenant, has come to an end" (Cyril of Jerusalem, 1975b: 188).

5. Irenaeus

Of a piece with Cyril's views are those of Irenaeus (c. 130–c. 200), who says of the sacraments that it was "indicated that the first people would cease to make offerings to God, but that in every place a sacrifice would be offered to him, and that a pure one; and that his name would be glorified among the nations" (Irenaeus: 184).

Hence "it is the Church's offering", and not Israel's, "which is counted as a pure sacrifice before God and which is acceptable to him". "The people of God *had* sacrifices and his Church *has* sacrifices" (Irenaeus: 185; emphasis ours). The new offerings are made by "free men" instead of "slaves", and these "free men" offer "their entire property" to the Lord instead of a mere tenth. When the Jews learned that they were not sacrificing rightly, "they were envious within. And so they murdered the righteous one, and rejected the advice of the Word, just as Cain had done" (Irenaeus: 185). No longer worshipping with the pure intention and sincere faith that characterizes the church, the Jews' "hands are full of blood" (Irenaeus: 186).

6. *Hippolytus*

Hippolytus (*c.* 179–*c.* 236), who lived and wrote in Rome, produced a liturgical treatise in which he detailed what was expected in the daily piety of the ordinary Christian. He instructs Christians to wash their hands and pray to God upon rising in the moring, to go to church if instruction in the Word is given on that day, to read at home from a holy book if it is not, to pray at the third, sixth and ninth hours and at midnight, and to make the sign of the cross on one's forehead whenever one is tempted. Yet he cannot spell out the daily round of the pious life without interlarding his prescriptions with anti-Judaism. The reason for praying at the third hour is that this "was the hour at which Christ was seen to be fastened to the tree" (Hippolytus: 207). And we should pray "powerfully" at the sixth hour, "imitating the cry of him who prayed and turned the whole creation to darkness for the unbelieving Jews" (Hippolytus: 207). Hippolytus insinuates anti-Jewish attitudes into the everyday life of pious Christians.

7. *Origen*

Origen (*c.* 185–*c.* 254) was born in Alexandria and succeeded Clement as head of the catechetical school there. Apparently he was the first preacher to establish the form of the homily as a continuous narrative on one particular passage of scripture. The homily at which we look here is on the Song of Solomon 1.1–12.

Commenting on the line, "I am very dark, but comely, O daughters of Jerusalem", Origen concludes that the bridegroom, Christ, loves the church more than he loves the daughters of Jerusalem. "Address yourself to the daughters of Jerusalem, you member of the Church, and say: 'The Bridegroom loves me more and holds me dearer than you, who are the many daughters of Jerusalem; you stand without and watch the Bride

enter the chamber' " (Origen: 45). This calls to Origen's mind
"the queen of the South" of Matthew 12.42, which says that
she "will arise at the judgment with this generation and
condemn it". Origen explains that "the queen of the South . . .
is the Church; and the men of this generation whom she
condemns, are the Jews, who are given over to flesh and blood"
(Origen: 45). She comes to hear the wisdom, not of Solomon,
but of Christ. Origen sanctions the church's role of condemning
Jews.

8. Ambrose

Ambrose (*c*. 339–*c*. 397) was Bishop of Milan in northern Italy
and is one of the four traditional doctors of the church. He was
famous as a preacher and upholder of orthodoxy and engaged
in several conflicts with the emperor, once excommunicating
Theodosius for a massacre (390). His sermon which we consider
here was preached on an earlier occasion.

In the year 388 the Christians of Callinicum, a town on the
Euphrates, had been goaded by their bishop to burn down a
synagogue. The Emperor Theodosius ordered the bishop to
rebuild it. In response, Ambrose wrote two letters. One was to
the emperor, contending that a Christian could not conceivably
erect a synagogue, that it could not be rebuilt with Christian
money, nor that of a Christian state. The second, to Ambrose's
sister, describes the sermon that Ambrose preached the next
time Theodosius attended church.

In the letter to Theodosius, Ambrose claims that he himself
is the offender: "I declare that I set fire to the synagogue, at
least that I instructed them to do it, that there might be no
place in which Christ is denied" (Ambrose: 232). He asks: "So
the unbelieving Jews are to have a place erected out of the spoils
of the Church? The patrimony acquired by the favour of Christ
for Christians is to be made over to the treasure of unbelief?"
(Ambrose: 232). He affirms that burning a single building is
unimportant, "and the less so when it was a synagogue that
was burnt, a place of unbelief, a home of impiety, a refuge of
insanity, damned by God himself" (Ambrose: 233–4). Not
content with vilifying the synagogue, Ambrose further charges

that the whole affair is one of the "tricks of the Jews, trying to bring a false charge" (Ambrose: 235). They do so because they want "to see row upon row of Christians in chains, the faithful with their necks under the yoke . . ." (Ambrose: 235). He pleads with Theodosius not to give this victory to the unbelieving Jews.

Ambrose's sermon to the emperor deals extensively with the story of Jesus' visit to the home of Simon, the Pharisee, for dinner (Luke 7.36–50). In the story, a woman of the city, a sinner, also comes, washes Jesus' feet with her tears, wipes them with her hair and anoints them with oil. Jesus tells Simon, his host, "You gave me no kiss, but from the time I came in she has not ceased to kiss my feet" (Luke 7.45).

The woman becomes "the church", and Simon becomes "the Jew". In the following remarks Ambrose contrasts the two. "It was because he had not a mind clean from the filth of unbelief that the Pharisee did not give Christ water for his feet" (Ambrose: 244). "A kiss is the sign of love. What kiss could the Jew have . . . ?" (Ambrose: 245). "The synagogue has no kiss. The Church has the kiss, the Church which waited for Christ, which loved him. . . ." "How can the Jew have this kiss?" "So the Pharisee had no kiss, except perhaps the kiss of the traitor Judas."

After his sermon, Ambrose went and stood before the emperor and refused to celebrate the eucharist until Theodosius promised to drop the whole affair (Ambrose: 249–50). By this time anti-Judaism is more than the internal rhetoric of the Christian community, shaping its character and social identity. Now it has a direct political impact, in this case legitimating the destruction of synagogues with impunity. Five years later, a new law had to be passed penalizing those who attacked synagogues, indicating that such attacks were on the increase.

9. Chrysostom

John Chrysostom (c. 347–c. 407) was known as "the golden-mouthed", as an acknowledgment of his ability as a Christian expositor. When his homiletical attention was turned to Jews, his "rhetoric could be poison-mouthed as well as golden-mouthed; certainly the most shocking of Chrysostom's works,

the *Homilies Against the Jews* . . . document the way Christian
rhetoric could serve as a vehicle for Christian anti-Semitism"
(Pelikan, 1967: 22).

Chrysostom's anti-Jewish rhetoric could surface no matter
what the topic of his sermon, as his homily on I Corinthians
10.16–17 attests. This homily is on two verses dealing with the
Lord's Supper. In it Chrysostom contrasts Christian worship
with Jewish, saying of the latter that "in the days of the old
covenant . . . he [God] was prepared to accept the blood which
they offered to idols" (Chrysostom, 1975: 198), alleging that
Jews worshipped idols. However, in the new covenant, God
"has provided in its place a far more awesome and glorious way
of worship" (Chrysostom, 1975: 198).

His anti-Jewish homilies "not only marked an important
moment in the Church's polemics against Judaism but they
seem to have exercised an influence which went far beyond
any specific occasion or local situation" (Harkins: xxxviii).
Chrysostom tells his hearers what occasions his concern: "The
festivals of the pitiful and miserable Jews are soon to march
upon us one after the other . . ." (Chrysostom, 1979: 3). Of his
congregants, some "will join the Jews in keeping their feasts
and observing their fasts" (Chrysostom, 1979: 4). He wishes to
"cure those who are sick with the Judaizing disease".

He calls the Jews "pitiable", because they "thrust aside" the
opportunity to accept Christ "and still sit in darkness. We, who
were nurtured by darkness, drew the light to ourselves and were
freed from the gloom of their error. They were the branches of
that holy root, but those branches were broken. We had no
share in the root, but we did reap the fruit of godliness"
(Chrysostom, 1979: 5). His displacement ideology surfaces in
this remark. In rejecting Christ, the Jews "grew fit for slaughter.
This is why Christ said: 'But as for these my enemies, who did
not want me to be king over them, bring them here and slay
them' " (Chrysostom, 1979: 8).

The synagogue is no better than a theatre, indeed it is worse,
being "not only a brothel and a theatre" but also "a den of
robbers and a lodging for wild beasts" (Chrysostom, 1979:
10–11). Hence God has abandoned the synagogue and forsaken

the people Israel (Chrysostom, 1979: 11). Citing John 8.19, Chrysostom contends that "no Jew adores God!" Nor is God worshipped in the synagogue.

Relations between ordinary Christians and Jews must have been cordial in fifth-century Antioch, and lay Christians knew little of any decisive break between the church and the synagogue. It is just this about which Chrysostom complains so vociferously: "Is it not strange that those who worship the Crucified keep common festival with those who crucified him?" (Chrysostom, 1979: 18). That ordinary Christians were theologically more generous than church leaders is a feature of the anti-Jewish literature going all the way back to Barnabas' complaint: "Do not become like some; do not add to your sins and say that the covenant is both their and ours. Yes! it is ours; but they lost it for ever when Moses had only just received it" (Barnabas: 195).

The only new aspect to Chrysostom's anti-Jewish preaching is the depth to which it descends. Its themes are the hackneyed motifs that still adorn Judaism. He shows us a Christian preacher striving to sever relations between Christians and Jews, to deprive the church of its Jewish legacy and Jews of their religious legitimacy, and to make an absolutist claim on behalf of the church, one grounded in works-righteousness: "we drew the light to ourselves".

An interim summing-up

A noted scholar of the early church brings to our attention the extremes to which anti-Judaism could go, quoting a Gnostic Christian, Saturninus, in second-century Antioch as saying: "Christ came to destroy the god of the Jews" (Grant: 107). For more orthodox Christians, the extreme versions of Gentile Christianity (such as Marcion's) were overcome differently: ". . . the God of the Hebrew Bible was 'salvaged' for Christians precisely by means of the anti-Judaic myth" (Efroymson, 1979: 101). Along with the rise in anti-Judaism went a loss of roots and memory: "To the Christian disciples of the first century the conception of Jesus as a rabbi was self-evident, to the

Christian disciples of the second century it was embarrassing, to the Christian disciples of the third century and beyond it was obscure" (Pelikan, 1985: 17). Anti-Jewish preaching did not cease in the early Middle Ages.

Reformation preaching

1. Zwingli

Ulrich Zwingli (1484–1531) began the Swiss Reformation in Zurich. His preaching attacked many aspects of the mediaeval church of which he disapproved. The sermon at which we shall look here, "On the Choice and Free Use of Foods", illustrates a tendency of Protestants to assail as "Jewish" everything they disliked about Christendom.

This sermon, based on Mark 7.15 ("there is nothing outside a man which by going into him can defile him"), articulates the entirely commendable point that we are not justified by abstaining from certain foods but by the grace of God. In making his point, however, Zwingli assumes as true the Gospel accounts of the Pharisees' anger at Jesus because of his desire to do away with "all the regulations" of the Torah (Zwingli: 98). He declares that the restrictions on foods in the Law are abolished because the law and the prophets "were only a symbol" and both "have been superseded" (Zwingli: 100). He interprets Paul as rejecting the Jewish idea that works are "a sure road to blessedness" and as accusing Jews of having given up trust in God and turning, with the heathen, to the "weak elements" (Zwingli: 106). Christ freed us "from all Jewish or human ceremonies" (Zwingli: 121). Christ here is not the one who brought the Gentiles near to Israel and made us "fellow citizens" with them in the household of God (Eph. 2.12, 19).

2. Luther

Martin Luther (1483–1546) founded the Reformation in Germany. Although the fundamental principles of his theology provide us with the central means to overcome anti-Judaism, a point which he himself sometimes made, he could be impetuous, rough and crude. He urged the opponents of the peasants to "smite, slay and stab" them, recommended executing the Anabaptists, and late in life advocated burning synagogues, destroying copies of the Talmud, and deporting all Jews from Germany (Williamson: 102).

In his sermon on the meaning of Pentecost, Luther differentiates "between our Pentecost and the Jewish Pentecost" (Luther, 1971: 48). The law prescribing their Pentecost is literal; ours is spiritual. Theirs, "since it is comprised only in writing and letters . . . was entirely dead; it also killed, and ruled a dead people" (Luther, 1971: 48). Jews cannot "cordially observe the commandments of God" (Luther, 1971: 48). Therefore the law "can make no one pious, or enter his heart" (Luther, 1971: 48). Our law is "spiritual, not written with pen or ink". Rather, at Pentecost "the Holy Spirit descended from heaven, and filled them all" (Luther, 1971: 48). We freely do God's will, as that is wrought in the heart by the Holy Spirit. "Now, all is life, light, understanding, will and heart, burning and delighting in all that is acceptable to God" (Luther, 1971: 49).

Luther's real target is not the Jews but what "the Pope establishes in his spiritless church" (Luther, 1971: 49). What is spiritual is here made "a mere outward matter, established in reference to external things and regulations". The medieval church creates "a dead written law" from what had been "the work of the Holy Spirit". "Thus, they make out of him a Moses, yes, mere human prattle" (Luther, 1971: 49). Luther attacks Christian practices that he does not like by labelling them as Jewish. Judaism symbolizes everything dead and literalist in religion.

Luther's series of sermons on the suffering of Christ illustrates how preaching on the texts and themes of Holy Week keeps alive strong anti-Jewish sentiment. Here, too, Luther's berating of the Jews is a way of criticizing the church of his day: "Just as Israel was heavily burdened with the ceremonial law, . . . so the papacy still conducts its divine worship" (Luther, 1956: 3).

Random assertions liberally distributed throughout these sermons accuse "the Jews" of all sorts of crimes against Jesus. "The godless Jews hurried Christ off to death . . ." (Luther,

1956: 216). "The Jews hated Jesus . . . [they] rejoiced in his misfortune . . ." (Luther, 1956: 163). The inscription above the cross "remains an eternal testimony against the Jews, that they could not rest until they had crucified their king" (Luther, 1956: 157).

Jesus compares the Jews "to an old, barren, dry and rotten tree, which is . . . only fit to be felled and burned" (Luther, 1956: 150). At Jesus' trial, the Jews cried out, "His blood be on us, and on our children", which " 'blood' began to flow down upon them in such streams that Jerusalem and the whole Jewish Kingdom soon were desolate . . . and it is now nearly fifteen hundred years, they have wandered about in misery, nowhere finding a continuing city" (Luther, 1956: 136). "The Jews to this day are labouring under the blood of Jesus Christ, and it will finally press them down to hell" (Luther, 1956: 137). The chief priests and elders "were moved against Christ by nothing but malice and envy" (Luther, 1956: 125), by a "savage, murderous hatred" (Luther, 1956: 94).

Luther's purpose, at least in part, is to prepare his followers for similar treatment: "But it is the manifest desire of the pope to treat us and the gospel as the Jews here treated Christ" (Luther, 1956: 75). Therefore, Luther urges his listeners to study carefully the trial and sufferings of Jesus: "For then, in case we are brought before a similar tribunal, we can follow the example of our Lord Jesus, learning of Him patience, and deriving from Him true consolation" (Luther, 1956: 80). Shamefully, Luther counselled his flock by attacking "the Jews".

Contemporary preaching

If anti-Judaism represents the past in Christian preaching, that past lives on in the present. Here we turn to consider a handful of journals containing the "best" in recent American preaching. The same sort of thing can doubtless be found elsewhere in the English-speaking world. Sermons published in such journals probably contain less anti-Judaism than one could expect to encounter from the pulpit generally. Yet it is present.

In a sermon on the need for saints, John Owen Gross states that all through his ministry Paul fought influences that would reduce Christianity "to an insipid Jewish cult" (*The Pulpit*, 1950: 11). The Jewish system, he avers, was built upon law, the Christian upon love; the Jewish is legalistic, but the Christian spirit is written upon the heart (*The Pulpit*, 1950: 11). Johnstone G. Patrick declares that "the scribes and Pharisees crucified our Lord, buried him, and securely sealed his sepulchre" (*The Pulpit*, 1950: 14).

Elden H. Mills has the chief priests, scribes and elders – "the best religious people of the hour" – "jibing" at Jesus, doing him to death, mocking and spitting upon him. "And then, having accomplished their bloody deed, while looking on to jeer, these best religious people went the limit of hypocrisy by flinging out the lie that they would believe him if he came down from the cross" (*The Pulpit*, 1950: 90). Edgar DeWitt Jones avers that "the climate of the New Testament is gentler and more favourable to justice tempered with mercy than the Old" (*The Pulpit*, 1950: 220) and passes on uncritically stories of Jesus' "accusers" who are interested only in trapping him (*The Pulpit*, 1950: 221). Francis J. McConnell speaks of "the Caesarea atmosphere, dominated as that was by a fiercely radical Jewish hatred", and declares that "the Jews" would have killed Paul if they had got a chance (*The Pulpit*, 1950: 230). In a Christmas sermon, Joseph S. Johnston explains that "Abraham, Jacob, Moses all knew what it was to be instructed by God. But instruction was partial, for their understanding was dull" (*The Pulpit*, 1950: 275). The law and the prophets were "all to little avail", so that at last God "came down to our dark world in the person of Jesus Christ" (*The Pulpit*, 1950: 275).

George H. Scherer, on the topic of spiritual freedom, claims that Jews who did not believe in Jesus "were the slaves of their theological creeds, their ecclesiastical prejudices, their ceremonial isolationism" (*The Pulpit*, 1951, 2: 10) and that since Jesus had condemned Pharisaism among the Jews he would not tolerate it among his disciples. Murray L. Wagner, preaching on the text, "You blind guides, straining out a gnat and swallowing a camel!" (Matthew 23.24), is trapped into the same kind of anti-Jewish tirade that Matthew 23 itself is. Jesus' accusers were "small potatoes", who "could never comprehend the expanse of his kingdom" (*The Pulpit*, 1951, 4: 9). Their contempt for him was because "he did not preach an old, worn-out religion. He came to declare a new way. The old had failed. Had the old religion been sufficient he would never have come as Lord" (*The Pulpit*, 1951, 4: 9). No wonder "they set about to rid themselves of him" (*The Pulpit*, 1951, 4: 9). They set out to ensnare him in his words, they were unconcerned with the multitudes of hungry people (*The Pulpit*, 1951, 4: 10). "They said, 'Let his blood be upon us and upon our children!' Their kind is always willing to have the children suffer the wretchedness imposed by small-potato minds" (*The Pulpit*, 1951, 4: 10).

Ralph W. Sockman proclaims that "in revealing God's character, Christ gave a distinctively new note" (*The Pulpit*, 1951, 8: 5). God no longer waits "to be approached and appeased by his creatures, but [is] . . . a divine shepherd going out to seek and save the lost" (*The Pulpit*, 1951, 8: 5). This accounts for why Christianity is a much more missionary religion than is Judaism: "In the Jewish view, God waits; in the Christian view, God seeks." Similarly, Edward L. R. Elson deplores the hypocrisy of the scribes and Pharisees and claims that at the time of Jesus Judaism "had long been without the ark, without the *Shechinah* [the presence of God]; now it is without the presence of Christ – without the favor of God. It was left to them desolate. In the end the rejection of God by his people and their renunciation of his ways led to national ruin" (*The Pulpit*, 1951, 10: 6). This ancient anti-Jewish theme is repeated, word for word, in this sermon.

In the mid 1960s, after the Second Vatican Council had instructed Roman Catholics on how preaching about Jews should be changed (Abbott: 660–688), anti-Judaism still continued to roll down like a mighty stream in Protestant preaching. Alfred T. Davies accused the best Jewish leaders of Jesus' day of superficiality, of plotting the death of Jesus, of censuring Jesus for healing a cripple and for forgiving sinners (*Pulpit Digest*, Jan. 1965: 37). From them he generalizes to "the Hebrew

people, God's people, who became so preoccupied with their
religion that they lost sight of their God" (*Pulpit Digest*, Jan.
1965: 38). Hence, "Jesus was killed by religion" (*Pulpit Digest*,
Jan. 1965: 40).

In a sermon on justice for American Blacks, Robert B.
Crocker proclaims that our attitudes towards Blacks should not
be like those of Jews towards Gentiles. He says that Barabbas,
the murderer, "was the son of a rabbi . . . brought up in a home
whose chief interest was religion" (*Pulpit Digest*, Feb. 1965: 31).
Barabbas was also a Zealot, fanatical in his "hatred of all those
who were non-Jewish" (*Pulpit Digest*, Feb. 1965: 31). Jesus, of
course, stood in "vivid contrast to Barabbas", utterly disregard-
ing "the restrictiveness of Judaism as an exclusive community"
(*Pulpit Digest*, Feb. 1965: 34). Today, the hated "Gentile is the
Christian Negro". Can Christians preach against prejudice
without preaching prejudice against Jews?

In a sermon discussing the congregation as a source of tension
for the clergy, Brewer L. Burnett looks at the congregations
where the gospel "ran into trouble" (*Pulpit Digest*, March 1965:
13). Congregations accused Jesus of blasphemy, of associating
with sinners, of breaking the law, of healing by the power of the
devil; they denied his authority to teach, sought to lay hands
on him, took up stones to cast at him, said that he was possessed
by a devil, sought to entangle him in his words, sought false
witnesses against him, spit on him, declared "let him be
crucified, and mocked him on the cross" (*Pulpit Digest*, March
1965: 13). All this transpired because Jesus "had uncovered
their pretensions". He scorned their love of the chief seats, of
long prayers, of covetousness, of hypocrisy, and opened "the
door for non-Jews" (*Pulpit Digest*, March 1965: 14). Burnett
takes comfort from Jesus' example: "Any man who is faithful
to the prophetic ministry . . . must inevitably learn to deal
constructively with controversy, tension, and, sometimes, open
hostility." The deep irony is his own failure to see that repeating
age-old anti-Jewish canards does not qualify one as a prophet.

In a 1965 sermon for Good Friday, Don D. Kaufman wonders
why Jesus "was not able to 'save himself' from" crucifixion. It
was not "because he lacked the skill or the strength to avoid

death at the hands of the Jewish people and the Roman soldiers" (*Pulpit Digest*, April 1965: 27). The answer lies in Jesus' preaching of the kingdom, in which "there was no place for the fulfilment of the political or nationalistic hopes of the Jews" (*Pulpit Digest*, April 1965: 27).

Two decades after the Second Vatican Council and four after Hitler's attempt to rid the earth of every last Jew, to make it "Judenrein" (clean of Jews), Protestant preachers in America tend to carry on the tradition of anti-Judaism, oblivious to its moral consequences. In a 1985 sermon on race relations, James P. Stobaugh deals with the story of Ruth, asking us to "call her a black person, a downstairs person" (*Pulpit Digest*, Jan.-Feb. 1985: 35). She could not glean from the fields – "a right normally reserved only for Jews". She was an outcast, a Moabite. He tells of a Grand Dragon of the Ku Klux Klan who sat next to his family at church, and of a young black man, Elias Brown, who was lynched for dating a white girl. Are Jews here being associated with the attitudes shown by the Klan? Did Christians learn racial prejudice from Jews? Did they not rather learn it from their own anti-Judaism?

In a 1985 Palm Sunday sermon, J. D. Glick wonders how the crowd that so enthusiastically welcomed Jesus to Jerusalem could make a radical about-face in only five days. Trying to understand "the dynamics of that week", he looks at the cleansing of the Temple, the cursing of the fig tree, the arguments with the Pharisees over taxes and with the Sadducees about resurrection, and Jesus' accusation of hypocrisy levelled at the Pharisees. "So, by the end of the week the crowd had turned against Jesus because he had so offended them with his actions and teachings" (*Pulpit Digest*, March-April 1985: 64, 65). Lent and Holy Week remain times when Christian preaching readily lapses into the accusatorial mode against the Jews.

Addressing the question of what was involved in the cleansing of the Temple, William E. Hull proposes that Jesus "carried the challenge of the kingdom to the apex of ecclesiastical power" (*Pulpit Digest*, Sept.-Oct. 1985: 14). His intention was "to reform the system as well as the individual", that is, "to destroy the Sanctuary itself", because it "stood condemned for its utter unworthiness to participate in the age to come, its colossal failure to be a house of prayer for all the nations" (*Pulpit Digest*, Sept.-Oct. 1985: 16). His goal was "to abrogate the entire system, root and branch". The Temple, barren as the fig tree, "had lost its very justification for existence" (*Pulpit Digest*, Sept.-Oct. 1985: 17). Jesus "rejected one Temple at the cost of his life that he might build out of his followers the true Temple of God" (*Pulpit Digest*, Sept.-Oct. 1985: 18). Jesus' followers – the church – are now the true temple; the old one, the Jewish people, being destroyed. The church, the new temple, "is to offer every person the opportunity to enter the immediate presence of God. In Judaism, only the qualified could seek God . . ." (*Pulpit Digest*, Sept.-Oct. 1985: 18). This sermon is ignorant of Judaism and supersessionist in its theology.

While preaching done by American Blacks has historically not been adequately represented in anthologies of sermons, this situation is changing somewhat. We are now able to read Black preaching and ask whether it is free from traditional anti-Judaism. Since Blacks have been themselves unjustly victimized by prejudice, one would expect their preaching to show a keen sensitivity to the situation of Jews, particularly after the Hitler era. Sadly, this does not seem to be the case.

Thelma Davidson Adair approvingly quotes Dean R. Hoge's contention that Jesus "opposed Jewish class distinctions and condemned the pretenses of the self-righteous who thanked God that they were not as other men" (Newbold: 20), without recognizing such criticism as Jewish self-criticism. Henry Bradford Jr suggests that religious complacency was typical of Jews. The Pharisee who thanked God that he was not as other men "was satisfied with his achievement and was thereafter complacent". The rich young ruler "went away sorrowful but he was satisfied even in his sorrow". "Felix, the great Jewish leader, was satisfied in his spiritual stagnation . . . Paul left him basking in his spiritual participation" (Newbold: 73).

Clinton M. Marsh, properly reminding us that God is the God of all nations and not merely of the Stars and Stripes, claims that "Israel spoke of a God of heaven and earth, but in reality saw Jehovah as its tribal God" (Newbold: 113). Gayraud

S. Wilmore says that Black people identify with Jesus "as the Oppressed Man of God", and refers to the crucifixion as the time "when the Nigger of Galilee was lynched in Jerusalem" (Newbold: 171), a reference hardly conducive to improved relations between Blacks and Jews.

Reviewing Black preaching here has the same function as reviewing other preaching – not to excoriate Blacks for anti-Judaism, but to show the continuing power of an unexamined ideology that is passed down from generation to generation. The ideology of anti-Judaism has always flourished in Christian groups that are or perceive themselves as oppressed. Such was the case with the church of the late first century, and there is no reason not to expect that it will remain so – until and unless we face up to the ideology of anti-Judaism itself.

Transition

This chapter has had the purpose of showing that, in fact, anti-Judaism not only was but remains a serious problem in Christian preaching. If we are to remove it, we must reach some understanding of how it originated, to which we now turn.

— 3 —

Anti-Judaism in the Canonical Literature of the Early Church

Introduction

In the previous chapter we saw that anti-Judaism is a frequent part of Christian preaching. A significant part of the reason for this development is the clear and unmistakeable appearance of anti-Jewish elements in the literature written by the early church and included in the canon. Indeed, a major purpose of some of this literature is to discredit and even defame Jewish people of the first century and their sacred institutions and practices. Each time such a passage is read from the Holy Bible in public worship, the reading has the effect of creating or reinforcing anti-Judaism and, ultimately, antisemitism.

Our purpose in this chapter is to help the reader become more sensitive to the anti-Jewish elements in the canonical documents. Space will not allow us to deal with each specific text or with every single issue, but we can get a sense of the lay of anti-Judaism in the theological land.

Before looking at the texts themselves, many of us need to acknowledge that we operate with a false picture of Judaism in the world of the first century. This picture has been – and continues to be – promulgated in Sunday School, in Christian preaching, in some seminary classrooms and in many commentaries, Bible dictionaries, theological word-books and other helps in biblical interpretation.

Put simply, the popular picture of first-century Judaism as a religion of legalism and works-righteousness is false. In this picture, Jews are depicted as staggering beneath the weight of at least 613 commandments which they must keep if they are to earn a place in the favour of God. God is a rigid, narrow, Great Accountant in the Sky, void of mercy and compassion, whose justice is largely retributive.

Fortunately, we now recognize this caricature as grossly inaccurate. And more and more Christian interpreters recognize Judaism in the world of the first century as a religion centred in a gracious, loving and forgiving God with the Torah seen as God's wonderful gift of instruction.

Yet old ways die hard. Even today materials appear from the best publishing houses which reinforce the old stereotype. Therefore, when using the secondary sources, as well as when reading the biblical text itself, readers will do well to practise suspicion and to ask a simple but revealing question. Is this evaluation of Judaism in this text historically accurate or does it result from the church's polemic against the Jews?

An issue with a long history in interpretation

The observation that anti-Judaism is found in the earliest documents from the hand of the church will be new to some readers. Therefore it is helpful to recall that this observation has appeared in modern scholarship for over seventy-five years. We mention here only a few representative voices.

By 1912, R. Travers Herford had noticed that the picture of the Pharisees in the Gospels was a distortion. Herford cautioned against using the Gospels as a source of reliable information about the Pharisees (Herford, 1912).

Although Rudolf Bultmann's writings continually presented the false picture of Judaism described above, he nonetheless noticed that many of the anti-Jewish sentiments in the present form of the synoptic tradition were either missing or greatly reduced in earlier versions of the material. In a representative controversy dialogue, Mark 3.1–6, Bultmann shows that the older part of the materials is 3.1–5, in which ". . . the opponents of Jesus are not described either as Scribes or Pharisees, but are unspecified". Only in the secondary v. 6 are the opponents of

Jesus identified as Pharisees (Bultmann, 1972: 52). According to Bultmann, the controversy was heightened as the synoptic tradition developed.

James Parkes pointed to a future emphasis among biblical interpreters when he noted that the bitter controversy between the synagogue and the nascent church was the seedbed in which the Gospels were written (e.g. Parkes, 1948: 48; cf. Parkes, 1934: 27–120, esp. 33–60; Parkes, 1947: 47–111). Parkes sees that the Gospel of John reads the enmity between the Johannine church and the synagogue in the late first century back into the life of Jesus in such a way ". . . that the Gospel embodies the interpretative expression of a memory and that the final relationship between the two parties is in memory hardened into antagonism from the outset" (Parkes, 1960: 222ff. cf. e.g. Brown, 1966: LXX–LXXV; Martyn, 1979).

Most significant biblical authorities in the mainstream of the Protestant and Catholic churches today agree that most of the unfavourable references to Jews and Judaism in the Gospels and Acts reflect the antagonism between Jews and Christians in the last third of the first century. Less consensus can be found among scholars on the relationship between Paul and Judaism, but even here we find trends in interpretation which help us look afresh at the position on Judaism and its relationship to Christianity which is taken in these writings.

In 1973, the highly respected Roman Catholic biblical scholar Gerard Sloyan's *Jesus on Trial* was published. Sloyan traces the development of the trial of Jesus in all four Gospels from the earliest traditions to their present adaptation in the four Gospels. Father Sloyan concludes that the earlier pieces of the trial stories were much less inimical to the Jewish community than our Gospels (Sloyan, 1973).

The most vigorous stimulus for re-examining the attitudes towards the Jews which are found in scripture has come from Rosemary Radford Ruether's *Faith and Fratricide* (1974). In a sizzling chapter, Ruether charges that the synoptics and Acts, Hebrews and the Fourth Gospel all explicitly reject Judaism. According to Ruether's interpretation, these early Christian writers see Christianity superseding Judaism. In the writings of Paul and Hebrews, this rejection was expressed in a "philosophizing mode", whereas in the Gospels it was expressed by intensifying the negative picture of the Jews and projecting the antipathy of the church of post-70 CE into the stories of the life of Jesus (Ruether: 64–116).

Samuel Sandmel, an eminent Jewish scholar, has gone through the literature of the early church with a fine toothcomb to bring together a detailed account of the instances of antisemitism in the New Testament (Sandmel, 1978). Many other interpreters are currently giving attention to the issue (e.g. Klein, 1978; Sloyan, 1978; Hare, 1979; Gaston, 1979; Townsend, 1979; Boadt, 1980; Fisher, 1983; Richardson, 1986).

No serious scholar seeking to identify anti-Jewish components in the sacred texts written by the early churches would say that these texts contain only rejection of Judaism. They contain the gospel message as well, and a gospel that can only be understood in the light of its Jewish background. But the fact is that many of the passages of the sacred literature from the pen of the early Christian communities distort and degrade Judaism. We look now at some key figures and books which figure in the history of anti-Judaism.

What about Jesus?

What was Jesus' attitude towards Judaism? The answer to this question is extremely problematic on two grounds – historical and theological.

The historical difficulty of identifying Jesus' attitude towards Judaism is that of determining the life and teaching of the historical Jesus. The primary sources of our knowledge of the historical Jesus are the four Gospels. Yet long ago scholars recognized that the picture of Jesus in the Gospels results almost entirely from the hand of the community and its experience with the risen Lord. Nonetheless, the critics concluded that several of the pericopae in the synoptic Gospels contain material which came from the life of the historical Jesus.

The question is, "What methodology can we use in order to recover materials from the historical Jesus?" The answer, posed in the sharpest and most enduring form by Rudolf Bultmann and followed by most major interpreters into the 1970s, is the criterion of dissimilarity, which is applied largely to the sayings attributed to Jesus. The operating principle of the criterion is very simple: if a saying is "dissimilar to the characteristic emphases both of ancient Judaism and of the early church" (Perrin, 1967: 39), then the saying may be regarded as coming from the historical Jesus. This criterion is supplemented by three other criteria: 1. coherence – that is, coherence with other material which has met the criterion of dissimilarity; 2. multiple attestation – that is, the multiple occurrence of material that has met the criterion of dissimilarity; 3. reflection of the environment of first-century Palestine. Not surprisingly, the picture of Jesus which results from the application of these criteria to the Gospel tradition is a picture of Jesus who is basically in conflict with the Jews of his day.

In recent years, a serious challenge has been given to this methodology and to the portrait of Jesus derived from it. Although Jesus grew up, lived and died as a Palestinian Jew among Palestinian Jews, the criterion of dissimilarity will not allow Jewish elements in its picture of the historical Jesus! Indeed, the dissimilar Jesus is almost ahistorical. Thus, the criterion of dissimilarity and the profile of Jesus derived from it violates one of the basic assumptions of the modern approach to the interpretation of history, namely, that the historian seeks to locate persons or events in the midst of the historical realities of their own times (Williamson, 1982: 11ff.).

In more recent years, scholars have recognized the importance of seeing Jesus as a Jew among Jews. Geza Vermes, for instance, argues that since Jesus' formative years were in Galilee, he would have been likely to be a Jewish leader of the type found in the first century, a charismatic miracle-working Rabbi (Vermes, 1974). E. P. Sanders, in the most important work on the historical Jesus in the 1980s, sees Jesus as prophetically acting out Jewish restoration eschatology which looked for a coming of God's new order (Sanders, 1985).

Both Vermes' Jesus and Sanders' Jesus are quite at home in first-century Judaism. Yet while the present search has much to commend it, its proponents have not agreed on a clear and crisp methodology for recovering the historical Jesus from the present heavily-interpreted Gospel materials. Nor have the modern authors' portraits emerged with the same Jesus.

What, then, can we say about Jesus' attitude toward Judaism? Acknowledging the difficulties of speaking with absolute certainty, many contemporary scholars think that Jesus was an itinerate miracle-worker and preacher whose message was centred on the coming rule of God. Like the Pharisees, Jesus is likely to have entered into discussion with other members of the Jewish communities on the issues of what it meant to be a faithful Jew and of how God was working in the world in order to be faithful to the divine promises. Where Jesus may have differed with his contemporaries on the interpretation of specific issues, he would be likely to have disagreed as a loyal member of the covenant community. But at present we can be more specific only with great caution.

In any case, a theological consideration enters the picture and seems to make the quest of the historical Jesus much less urgent. The Jesus who is decisive for the church is the risen, living Lord and not the historical Jesus. After the death of Jesus, it was not Jesus' teaching or moral example which energized the disciples; according to the earliest witnesses (e.g. I Cor. 15.3–4) it was the experience of the resurrected Jesus in their midst. From that day until this, then, a central part of the work of the church is to reflect upon the significance of the risen Jesus as a paradigmatic disclosure of the character of God and of the purpose of God in the world. Thus the real question is not "What was Jesus' attitude towards the Jews of his day?" The real question is, "What does the living Jesus disclose to the present church about God's attitude towards the church's anti-Judaism . . . and about those elements of scripture which are anti-Jewish?"

The death and resurrection of Jesus disclose God's infinite love for each and all. Anti-Judaism denies that love to Jewish people. Therefore anti-Judaism is inappropriate *wherever* it is found.

Homiletical preoccupation with the life and teaching of Jesus often results in a picture of Jesus who is a wise teacher and moral example but who no longer has the power of a saviour over sin and death. Such preaching is spiritually dry and moralistic. Furthermore, such concentration often leads to historical anachronism – reading a modern concern into the ancient text. Thus the preacher sometimes caricatures the historical Jesus as a feminist, as a civil rights leader, as a Marxist. The historical Jesus then functions as a kind of "proof-text" for the contemporary agenda. This is bad history and bad theology. Instead, preachers who turn their attention to the risen Jesus whose presence is still with the church will find a Jesus who is authentically contemporary and a powerful saviour.

Paul and the great misunderstanding

Paul wrote more letters and influenced more letters than any other contributor to the little library contained in the Bible. These writings contain considerable reflection on the relation-ship between Jews and Christians, and the church's interpre-tation of these reflections has had considerable import in shaping its attitude toward Judaism. In coming to terms with Paul, the interpreter needs to take account of five significant matters.

First, we who have been influenced by the Reformation need to become critical of the commonly held Reformation interpretation of Paul. For the churches influenced by the Reformation, Paul's doctrine of justification by grace has functioned as a "canon within the canon". The contrasting doctrine which Paul is said to oppose is justification by works, a position frequently attributed to the Jews and to Paul's Judaizing opponents. Paul preaches grace where the Jews advocate legalism. To the present day, much preaching and scholarship in the Reformation tradition perpetuates this view (e.g., Bultmann, 1951: 185ff. Käsemann, 1980).

This little summary does not represent the richness and complexities of the Reformation views. But it does encapsulate a popular understanding of Paul which is often *assumed* when preachers come to Paul. The insight that justification is by grace alone is infinitely commendable as a theological position. But the simple polarization of Christianity (grace) and Judaism (work) can no longer be defended. For this polarization is based on a false understanding of Judaism (pp. 28–9 above) and on a misreading of Paul's own statements.

Secondly, the picture of Paul in Acts needs to be left behind when one is seeking the attitude of the historical Paul toward Judaism. The stories of Paul in Acts are a vehicle for the presentation of Lucan theology. A careful study of the picture of Paul in Acts will help fill out the profile of Luke's attitude towards the Jews and Judaism of his own day, but will reveal very little about the historical Paul.

Thirdly, we need to remember that Paul's letters were written over a long period of time and that Paul's mature thought on a subject should always be taken into account in preaching and teaching. Interpreters today are agreed that Romans 9–11 is Paul's most fully developed statement on the relationship between things Jewish and things Christian. Earlier passages on this subject need to be brought into dialogue with the trenchant passages in Romans.

Fourthly, as Galatians 1.11–17, esp. vv. 15–16 makes clear, Paul understood his calling to be that of apostle to the Gentiles. In a widely approved essay, Krister Stendahl points out that Paul never speaks of his conversion from Judaism to Christianity. Instead, Paul speaks of a call; both before and after his call as apostle to the Gentiles, Paul served the same God. Where once he served God within the community of Judaism, his vocation (calling) is now to serve God among the Gentiles (Stendahl, 1976). Note that Paul describes his call in language which evokes the calls of Isaiah 49.1–6 (esp. v. 1) and Jeremiah 1.4–19 (esp. v. 4), both of whom speak of the importance of their work to the Gentiles.

To be sure, "Godfearers" and some regular Jews came into fellowship with the congregations to whom Paul wrote, but Paul clearly regards the main constituents of these congregations as Gentiles who have turned away from false religions to the living God (e.g. I Thess. 1.9; I Cor. 12.2; Gal. 4.8; Rom. 1.5–6).

Nowhere does Paul speak of himself as a teacher whose arena is Israel. Galatians 2.11–21 is crucial in this regard. For here Paul reports the recognition of his ministry by the Jewish-Christian community at Jerusalem and the agreement reached between himself and the Jerusalem community. "And when they perceived the grace that was given to me, James and Cephas and John, who were reported to be pillars, gave to me and Barnabas the right hand of fellowship that we should go to the Gentiles and they to the circumcised" (Gal. 2.9). Deeply influenced by apocalyptic, Paul ultimately understands the coming of the Gentiles to God to be eschatological (e.g. Romans 11.25–36; 15.26–27).

Paul evaluates his experience in Judaism very positively. Krister Stendahl calls attention to the robust character of this apostle's fullest autobiographical comment on his life prior to his call to preach to the Gentiles, Philippians 3.4–6.

> If any other man thinks he has reason for confidence in the flesh, I have more: circumcised on the eighth day of the people of Israel, of the tribe of Benjamin, a Hebrew born of the Hebrews; as to the law, a Pharisee, as to zeal a persecutor of the church, as to righteousness under the law blameless.

The literary context of this passage (3.1–16) is one of polemic against intruders who have come into the Gentile Philippian community and called for the Gentiles to accept Jewish practices. In strong language (3.2), Paul opposes any suggestion that Gentile Christians at Philippi should adopt Jewish practices, but the apostle does not denigrate Judaism as such. Nor, for that matter, does he ever say that he regrets being a Jew. About his life prior to his call as an apostle he has but one sorrow, namely that he persecuted the church (Gal. 1.14–15).

Fifthly, we always need to keep in mind that Paul's statements about Jewish customs and beliefs, especially about the law, are directed to congregations largely composed of Gentile Christians. Paul is clearly not speaking to Jews about the validity of their religious experience. Rather, as Lloyd Gaston points out, the apostle is ". . . dealing with Gentile-Christian problems, foremost among which was the right of Gentiles *qua* (as) Gentiles, without adopting the Torah of Israel, to full citizenship in the people of God" (Gaston, 1979: 56).

Paul's position is at heart quite simple. Gentile Christians need not adopt Jewish practices in order to be considered full members of the household of God. Gentile Christians come to God through Christ in a way which is parallel to the way in which Jews come to God through the Torah.

> The Gentile counterpart to living in the covenant community of Torah is being "in Christ". Christ is the fulfillment of the promise concerning the Gentiles given to Abraham. God shows his righteousness, his faithfulness to his promise in a new act, apart from the Sinai covenant but not contradictory to it (Romans 3.21) (Gaston, 1979: 65).

Both Jew and Gentile, under the power of sin, are redeemed by grace.

Why, then, the great misunderstanding of Paul? And why do several passages, notably in Galatians and Romans, seem to cast a dark shadow over Judaism and especially over the law?

Members of Paul's communities have encountered a law-observant gospel and have begun to observe Jewish law. J. Louis Martyn argues convincingly that, at least in the case of Galatia, the law-observant gospel has come from teachers who are "embarked on an ecumenical mission under the genuine conviction that, through the law of his Messiah, God is reaching out for the Gentiles and thus for the whole of humankind" (Martyn, 1983: 228). The example *par excellence* is circumcision (6.12). Martyn is careful to point out that the law-observant mission to the Gentiles is likely not to be a direct reaction to Paul's law-free mission. Elsewhere, the preachers of the law-observant movement ". . . will have worked virgin fields impelled not by a desire to correct Paul but by a passion to share with the entire world the only gift they believed had the power to liberate humankind from the grip of evil, the Law of the Messiah" (Martyn, 1983: 235). Regardless of motive and circumstance, however, Paul objects that observance of the law is not appropriate for Gentile Christians who have come to know God through Jesus Christ. And when Paul's passions are aroused, he can engage in mud-slinging which, Martyn reminds us, ". . . one commonly finds among competitive preachers, especially, but not exclusively, in the Hellenistic age" (Martyn: 230).

Lloyd Gaston points out that Paul uses the one Greek word *nomos* (law) in two senses:

1. As Torah, it refers to covenantal relationship with God. For Jews, this relationship is defined at Sinai. When so used, *nomos* is a strong and positive word. In Galatians 6.2, for instance, Paul can say "Bear one another's burdens and so fulfil the Torah of Christ" (Gaston, 1979: 58–9, 62ff.).

2. But in some passages Paul uses the word *nomos* in a decidedly negative way. Following a tradition prevalent in the apocrypha and pseudepigrapha, Paul uses "law" in these passages to refer to the hopeless situation of the Gentiles who have not been obedient to God. In this frame of reference, law (*nomos*) functions only to condemn Gentiles. Although Gentiles did not have access to the commandments of God through the revelation at Sinai, God's ways were still revealed to them through Adam and through Noah, but humankind chose to disobey God. Only thus can Paul speak of people as "under the law", i.e. not under Torah but under condemnation! This is the sense in which Paul says: "For sin will have no dominion over you, since you are not under law (i.e. condemnation) but under grace" (Rom. 6:14) (Gaston, 1979: 59–64).

One obvious implication for the preacher is the necessity of determining how Paul is using the word law in specific contexts. Is it Torah? Or is it condemnation?

Paul's concern is for the Gentile Christians to see that, by virtue of God's action in Jesus Christ, they are no longer under condemnation but are children of grace. According to Galatians 3 and Romans 4, the Gentile Christians are now heirs of the promises of God to Abraham and Sarah. According to Romans 9–11 these promises are still valid for the Jews, too.

Of course, Paul is aggravated that the Gentile Christians have been disturbed. And he responds with conviction and even fire. But his response is not anti-Judaism. Quite the opposite: ". . . Paul said nothing against Torah and Israel, but simply by-passed them as irrelevant to his gospel" (Gaston, 1979: 66; cf. Sanders, 1977; 1983).

Conflict between church and synagogue reflected in the Gospels

One of the great discoveries of the modern study of the Gospels is that they reflect the situations of the churches to which they were written. Stories and sayings about Jesus have been arranged, adapted (sometimes radically), drawn from early Christian prophets, and even created by the authors, in order to speak directly to their communities. The four Gospels are not "biographies of Jesus" in the contemporary sense, but are much more like narrative sermons addressed to specific developments in the churches.

One of the developments which is common to the communities of Matthew, Mark, Luke and John is conflict between Jews and Christians. In this respect, the early churches found themselves in a peculiar position. On the one hand, their roots and basic interpretative categories came from Judaism. Yet particularly after the fall of Jerusalem, and as the Gentile mission expanded, the church found itself in growing conflict with representatives of the very religious group from which it came. This peculiarity is reflected in all four Gospels: appreciation and appropriation of aspects of Jewish theology, yet deprecation of Jews and even of Judaism. The nuances of the conflict are different in the case of each Gospel.

The point to be made clear now is that the Gospel writers projected their attitudes toward the Jews of their own day on to the picture of the Jews in the Gospels. This is especially true of the leaders of the Jews, such as the Pharisees, the scribes and the priests. The Pharisees in the Gospel of Mark, for instance, are not historical Pharisees from the days of Jesus but represent Mark's evaluation of the Jews of his own day, *circa* 70 CE. For instance, in those passages in which Sabbath observance is an issue (e.g. Mark 2.23–3.6), the issue is between the church of Mark and the Jews of his own day. Mark presents his position on the issue through the drama of Jesus and the Pharisees.

1. The Gospel of Mark: the Jews as possessed by demons

Mark's Gospel has rightly been called an "apocalyptic drama" (Perrin and Duling, 1982: 233). Mark's underlying theology is the two-age dualism of apocalypticism in which history is seen as divided into two ages. The old age is a time of brokenness, sin and death ruled over by Satan and the demons. This old epoch has now been invaded by Jesus who announces the inbreaking of the new age (RSV: kingdom) (e.g. Mark 1.14–15). Thus the underlying plot of the gospel drama is the conflict between God – and God's agent Jesus – and the devil whose agents are the demons.

According to Mark, the Jews are possessed by demons and therefore, belong to the old age. In the early parts of the Gospel, the leaders of the Jews (especially the scribes and Pharisees) are pictured as possessed. But by the time of the condemnation of Jesus to death the masses themselves are pictured as belonging to Satan.

This aspect of the Marcan story-line begins in 1.21–28, where the first Jewish institution is mentioned – a synagogue at Capernaum. Inside the synagogue is someone with an unclean spirit, i.e. possessed by a demon. The reader is left with the impression that the synagogue is a habitation of the demon possessed.

The first overt conflict between Jesus and the Jewish leaders is 2.1–12, when Jesus is accused of blasphemy (2.7). The pattern of opposition continues through 2.15–3.61.

3.20–29 is a key passage. The scribes charge that Jesus is possessed by demons (v. 22). Yet Jesus reasons, "How can Satan cast out Satan?" Further, ". . . if a house is divided against itself, that house will not be able to stand. And if Satan has risen up against himself, he cannot stand, but is coming to an end" (vv. 25–26). Whose house, in this Gospel, is divided against itself and therefore reveals itself to be a house of Satan which cannot stand? Clearly, it is the Jews. For at the trial of Jesus, ". . . many bore false witness against him, *and their witness did not agree*" (14.56; cf. vv. 57–59). And in order to make the point even more explicit, Mark points out that those who blaspheme against the Holy Spirit cannot be forgiven but are guilty of an eternal sin (3.28–29). Blasphemy against the Holy Spirit is declaring that Jesus has an unclean spirit (3.30), and the only ones in this Gospel to make that statement are the Jews.

Jewish unbelief prevents Jesus from working miracles in 6.1–6. In 6.14–27, Mark reveals the character of the political leadership of the Jews by depicting Herod as the heartless murderer of John the Baptist (6.14–28), a judgment with which many Jews would have agreed. Mark 7.1–23 declares Jewish practices to be completely obsolete, and, indeed, superficial. ". . . there is nothing outside a man which, by going into him, can defile him; but the things which come out of a man are what defile him" (7.16).

Chapter 8 is remarkable for its diminution of the Jews. In 8.11 the Pharisees come to *test* Jesus. Those who read the Greek Bible immediately recognize the same word here (*peirazein* as in 1.13, where Jesus was "tempted" (*peirazein*) by the devil! The Pharisees are thus shown to be in league with Satan. In 8.15 Jesus cautions the disciples (who do not come off so well in this Gospel) to beware of the leaven of the Pharisees and Herod. Leaven here may be a Jewish idiom for the evil tendency in humankind (Cranfield, 1963: 260).

The withering of the fig tree (11.12–14 and 11.20–25) is a kind of "action parable" of the temple and its fate. The temple is a fig tree without figs. No longer a house of prayer, it has become a den of robbers (11.15–19). Therefore the temple and all it represents will wither under the curse of God. In 11.20, the reader is admonished to have faith in God, not in the temple.

The parable of the vineyard (12.1–12) does not develop the theme of demonic possession, but its verdict on the Jews is hardly more hopeful. "What will the owner of the vineyard do? He will come and destroy the tenants (i.e. the Jews) and will give the vineyard to others (i.e. the church)" (12.9).

The anti-Jewish elements in Mark become most marked in the passion story. The chief priests, scribes and elders send "a crowd with swords and clubs" to arrest Jesus (14.43–49). On the basis of the scantiest evidence ". . . they all condemned him as deserving death. And some began to spit on him and cover his face and strike him, saying, 'Prophesy!' " (14.64b–65). The leaders of Israel are responsible for taking him to Pilate and for the release of Barabbas. For ". . . the chief priests stirred up the crowd to have him (Pilate) release for them Barabbas instead" (15.11). In 15.13–14, the crowd is depicted as "crying out" (13) and "shouting" (14). This may suggest that the crowd itself is possessed. The same Greek word is translated by "cry out" and "shout" (*krazo*), and several other times in Mark *krazo* is used to describe the behaviour of those who are possessed by demons. They cry out (1.24, 26; 3.11; 5.5, 7; 9.26, but contrast 6.49; 9.24; 10.48; 11.9 (?); 15.39).

At the cross, the chief priests and scribes mock the dying Jesus (15.31). And the final Marcan comment on Judaism is the rending of the veil of the temple (15.38), which makes the temple impotent. Henceforth, for Mark, the temple is an empty bank.

2. Matthew and ambivalence towards Judaism

Matthew's attitude towards Jews and Judaism is the most ambivalent of the four Gospels. Clearly Matthew's roots are deep in Jewish soil. Matthew employs Pharisaic modes of thinking and arguing so extensively that it may even be possible to speak of Matthew as a Christian Pharisee.

Yet Matthew is a Jewish *Christian* whose community is in tension with Jews, perhaps even with the Pharisees. For Matthew, one of the critical issues facing his church is the same as that facing the Pharisees: authentic interpretation. Who is the rightful interpreter and what is the rightful interpretation of the traditions of Israel? The Sermon on the Mount, for instance, is a casebook of Jewish expression and is even organized around a fundamental image of the Jewish vocation: "You are the light of the world" (5.14).

From the beginning of the Gospel, Matthew is clear that the Jewish traditions can be fully understood only in the light of the fulfilment of its promises in Jesus. And *vice versa*, Jesus can be understood only in the light of the sacred scriptures of Israel.

Jesus and the mission to the Gentiles are the natural destiny of the promises of God (Matt. 1.1–17; 2.1–12; 5.12–17, etc.).

Matthew's negative thesis is that the Jews of Matthew's day have not rightly understood God's work in Jesus and in the church. In fact the Jews have not understood their own Bible rightly and have resisted the work of God. The Jews are not possessed, as they are in the Gospel of Mark, but they fail to see the validity of the church.

The polemic begins in chapter 2 in the contrast between the pagan astrologers who worship the baby Jesus with their wonderfully symbolic gifts (see Isaiah 60.8) and King Herod, the only Jew to pay attention to the birth of Jesus.

John the Baptist condemns the Pharisees and Sadducees as "You brood of vipers", a charge which is repeated in 12.24 and 23.33. The implication is that they are not children of God but are children of the snake of Genesis 3. Nonetheless, their case is not hopeless, for they can repent (3.7–10).

Matthew uses Jewish materials in the Sermon on the Mount in such a way as to show that they belong to the church. For example:

You (the church) are the salt of the earth (5.13).
You (the church) are the light of the world (5.14).

According to Matthew, the interpretation of Jesus is the means whereby the intention of the law and the prophets can be fulfilled (5.17–48), and Matthew is directly critical of the interpretation of the scribes and the Pharisees (5.20). Chapter 6 is a litany of laments against the piety practised by the Jews of Matthew's day. These Jews are "hypocrites" who love to make a public display with their prayer, their almsgiving and their fasting. Matthew's objection is not to the Jewish practices themselves, but to the way in which the Jews of his own day carried them out. Indeed, Matthew's community is given explicit instructions in how to be more Jewish than the Jews (6.3, 6, 9, 17).

Given this view of Judaism, no wonder Matthew takes up a traditional Jewish image for the criticism of religious leadership when he says that the crowds are like "sheep without a shepherd" (9.36; cf. Ezekiel 34; Jeremiah 23.1–14; Zechariah 10.2ff.). The Pharisees are not fit shepherds. This theme permeates the Gospel (e.g. 12.6–7, 34, 39–41, 45; 15.13–14, where the Pharisees are called "blind guides"; 16.5–11; 23.1–39).

The mission of Jesus is first to the lost sheep of the house of Israel (10.6), but because these lost sheep are really wolves (10.16), the Twelve can expect to be delivered up in councils and flogged in synagogues (10.17), a legal means of synagogue discipline. From this vantage point, Matthew's comment is poignant. "For my yoke is easy and my burden is light" (11.30). Since the "yoke" is a Rabbinic symbol of the law, the reference may be a claim that the yoke (i.e. law) of Jesus is easier (read: better) than the yoke of the Pharisees.

The parable of the labourers in the vineyard is an excellent example of Matthean ambivalence (20.1–16). The story is an allegory about Jews and Gentiles in which the Jews (the workers hired early in the day) grumble about the inclusion of the Gentiles (the workers hired at the eleventh hour). However, despite the grumbling the householder does not cut off the workers who were hired in the early part of the day.

After Jesus' entry into Jerusalem, Matthew's animosity towards the Jews heightens. The chief priests and the scribes are indignant when Jesus is praised by the children as the Son of David. Jesus responds that the words of the children are "perfect praise" (2.16), again implying that the thrust of Jewish history is now turning towards the church and away from those who do not recognize Jesus.

The Jews are like the child who promised to work in the vineyard but did not (21.28–32); like the tenants who killed the heir (21.33–43); like the guests who refused to come to the banquet or who came in the wrong dress (22.1–13).

The Jews, especially the Pharisees, are then said to resolve to entangle Jesus in his own talk (22.15). But alas, they are the ones who become entangled, and provide Jesus with the occasion for the bitterest invective against the Scribes and Pharisees in the Gospel, Matthew 23. Matthew does give a forthright endorsement of the *teaching* of the Pharisees when he says: "The scribes and Pharisees sit on Moses' seat; so practise and observe whatever they tell you, but not what they do; for they preach but do not practise" (23.2–3). The problem is not with Jewish tradition and belief but with the Pharisees of Matthew's generation who are depicted as grossly misunderstanding the commands of God, as blind guides, whose blindness led to the shedding of the innocent blood of the prophets, wise ones and scribes (23.29–36), as well as to the scourging and persecution of some of the members of Matthew's church (23.34). Matthew concludes the attack by vindictively wishing upon the Pharisees responsibility for "all the righteous blood shed on earth" (23.35). The role of the Jews in the trial of Jesus is described in Chapter 5 (pp. 85ff.).

Ironically, Matthew's own theology contains seeds which reject anti-Judaism. For instance, Matthew contains an important emphasis on reconciliation between enemies and on forgiveness (e.g. Matt. 5.21–26; 18.10–35). This is part of what it means to be the light of the world.

3. *The long journey to the abandonment of the Jews in Luke-Acts*

Although Luke has considerable sympathy for Jewish customs and even some Jews, he sees the future of the church as one in which Jewish practices will play little part. The conclusion results not from a penetrating Lucan critique of Judaism as such but from the Jewish rejection both of Jesus and of the gospel preached by the Lucan church. In consequence, Luke-Acts begins by fully embracing Judaism but ends in the abandonment of the Jews by the church.

An inviolate axiom when working with the writings of Luke is always to see Luke-Acts as one work. Each pericope is to be interpreted in the light of its place in the whole story. Only thus can Luke's use of a passage come into full view.

Luke is clear that Jesus, and hence the Christian mission, originated among Jews (Luke 1–2). Scholars typically observe that Mary, the young Jewish woman, is for Luke a model of the faithful response to the initiatives of God. "Behold, I am the handmaid of the Lord; let it be to me according to your word" (1.38). The major interpretative categories by which Jesus is explained are Jewish in origin or style, including the presage of the Gentile mission (e.g. 2.29–32).

When Jesus arrives at the synagogue in Nazareth (4.14–30), he enters fully into the Sabbath service. The rub comes when Jesus applies the prophecy of Isaiah 60.1–2 to the Gentiles by citing two examples: God's providence visited upon the widow of Zarephath (a woman, a widow, a Gentile!) and upon Naaman the Syrian; on neither occasion was the providence of God visited upon a Jew. The conclusion of the story prefigures a major part of the Lucan analysis of the Jewish response to Jesus and the church: "When they (the synagogue crowd) heard this, all in the synagogue were filled with wrath. And they rose up and put him out of the city" (4.28–29). After 4.1–30 and 5.17–6.11, the reader is not surprised when Jesus accuses Jewish leaders of rejecting the purposes of God (7.29–30) and of having second-rate love for God (7.41–43). Indeed, the Jewish love for God is inferior to that given by a woman who was a sinner.

The Gospel's complaint against Jews comes to its most aesthetic and memorable expression in the Lucan parables. The parable of the Good Samaritan attacks priests and levites (Luke 10.29–37). At a dinner party, Jesus is clear that the Pharisees have rejected the initiatives of God while the sick and outcast have accepted (14.1–24, esp. vv. 15–24).

The sullen older brother is a classical Lucan caricature of Judaism. When he heard the music and dancing of the party celebrating the return of the profligate younger son, the older brother became angry and refused to go into the house. The father insists that nothing has been taken from him: ". . . all that is mine is yours". As the interpreters of the parable are fond of pointing out, the story ends with the door to the party still open. The reader does not know whether the elder brother goes in, and hence the readers must decide for themselves whether they will enter. But according to the later testimony of Acts, the older brother has certainly made the decision to stay away (15.11–32). Other parables manifest similar emphases (e.g. 16.19–31; 18.9–14; 19.11–27, esp. 27; 20.9–19).

On the journey to Jerusalem (9.51–19.27), the Jewish leaders become more hostile to Jesus and they begin to think of what to do with Jesus. Jesus continues to criticize them and to warn his disciples (11.14–23, 29–32, 37–53; 12.1–3, 18–12 esp. 11, 49–53, 54–59; 13.6–9, 10–17 [an important passage], 31–35 esp. 34–35; 16.14–15; 17.11–19).

Careful use of a synopsis, comparing the versions of Mark, Matthew and Luke, shows that in Jesus' encounter with the Jews in Jerusalem Luke has lessened the Jewish role in the death of Jesus. For instance, Judas no longer operates under his own authority but is under the control of Satan (22.3–6), and the trial scene before the assembly is considerably abbreviated (22.66–71). Herod, whom even the Pharisees dislike (13.31), is given a prominent role in the decision to put Jesus to death (23.6-12). Luke in fact presents the least anti-Jewish version of the trial and death of Jesus. Still, the Jews figure prominently in the proceedings, esp. in 19.47–48; 20.19–26, 45–57; 22.47–53, 66–71; 23.1–5, 6–12, 13–25.

In Acts, Luke's anti-Jewish sentiments are displayed primarily in two ways: 1. Through statements put into the mouths of the apostles and other leaders of the church; 2. Through descriptions of Jewish reactions to the preaching of the gospel and the life of the church, especially its Gentile witness.

The coming of the Spirit and the constitution of the church on the day of Pentecost has both a positive and a negative aspect *vis-à-vis* the Jews (Acts 2.1–42). On the one hand, Pentecost is a Jewish holy day; the language and imagery of the coming of the Spirit is all of Jewish origin and the story of the tower of Babel (which is the conscious foil to the story of Pentecost) is a Jewish story. But the narrative implicitly suggests that the Spirit has been transferred to the church (2.17–18, 23).

The speakers of the church repeatedly accuse the Jews of the death of Jesus. Stephen, the first to follow Jesus in martyrdom, is also first in rank in anti-Judaism. At the climax of the Lucan rendition of the history of Israel, Stephen declares, "You stiff-necked people, uncircumcised in heart and ears, you always resist the Holy Spirit. As your fathers did, so do you. Which of the prophets did not your fathers persecute? And they killed those who announced beforehand the coming of the Righteous One, whom you have now betrayed and murdered" (7.51–52).

The speakers in Acts clearly hold the Jews primarily responsible for the death of Jesus (cf. 2.22–36; 3.11–26; 4.5–12, 23–31; 5.27–32; 10.34–43; 13.26–43). In the later materials in Acts the Jews are pictured as trying to kill Paul, the great missionary to the Gentiles.

The Jews repeatedly misunderstand the preaching of the church, harass its witnesses, and even bring legal proceedings against them. Peter and John are arrested by the temple executives when the apostles preach the resurrection of Jesus from the dead (4.1–22). Filled with jealousy, the high priest and Sadducees put the apostles in prison. The impotence and infidelity of the priests is revealed when an angel opens the prison doors. This pattern continues throughout Acts. Stephen, for instance, is stoned, apparently with official approval (6.8–8.1; cf. 9.23–25; 12.1–19; 13.44–52; 15.19–23).

The vivid narrative of Paul's call is designed to show that Paul's mission to the Gentiles is of divine origin. The imagery of the light and the voice recall the theophanies of the history of Israel (9.3–5). The commission itself is spoken in Septuagintal language (9.15–16). The importance of this story to Luke is revealed in the fact that he tells it *three* times (9.1–22; 22.4–16; 26.9–18).

After several unpleasant encounters with Jews, Paul has had enough. When the Jews at Corinth ". . . opposed and reviled him, he shook out his garments and said to them, 'Your blood be upon your heads. I am innocent. From now on I will go to the Gentiles' " (18.6). Similar incidents dog the rest of the Lucan portrayal of the Pauline ministry, e.g. 18.8–10, 21–41 esp. 33; 20.17–35 esp. 19. The Jews are responsible for the arrest that finally gets Paul sent to Rome. Note, too, the prominence of the Jewish leaders in the maltreatment of the missionary to the Gentiles in 21.27–23.30; 23.31–24.27; 24.24–25.5, 6–12, 13–22, 23–26.30; 28.17–29. At the end of the book of Acts, Paul makes the definitive Lucan statement on the relationship between the Jews and the Christian church. "Let it be known to you, then, that this salvation of God has been sent to the Gentiles; they will listen" (28.28). The heart of the Jews of Luke's day has grown dull (28.27).

Despite this final rejection, Luke's sensitivity to Judaism can be seen in two important passages. In Acts 10–11, Peter is given a vision by which all foods are declared clean. There is no explicit polemic against the dietary laws as such, nor does Luke make an attack upon the Jews for hypocrisy in observing such laws or in confusing external ceremony with matters like justice and mercy. The vision is simply a way of indicating the divine approval of the Gentile mission. And in the so-called Apostolic Council Luke is perfectly willing to acknowledge the validity of Jewish practices and yet to abridge these practices for Gentiles (15.1–35). And throughout the Pauline mission a few Jews are depicted as responding positively to Paul's preaching and coming into the church.

4. John and the replacement of Judaism by the church

Interpreters commonly and correctly note that anti-Judaism in the Gospels is most savage in the Fourth Gospel. Three observations bring this situation into clear focus.

First is the Johannine world-view. John's universe is divided into two spheres: *heaven* (the home and domain of God) and *earth* (the home and domain of the forces hostile to God). The Johannine world-view and some of the characteristics of the two spheres of existence are represented in the following diagram:

GOD
(heaven)

grace	spirit	life	truth	light	belief	church

law	flesh	death	falsehood	darkness	unbelief	Jews

DEVIL
(darkness)

The Jews belong to the lower sphere of existence, as John states quite explicitly in 8.12–59. "Why," Jesus asks the Jews, "do you not understand what I say? It is because you cannot bear to hear my word. You are of your father the devil, and your will is to do your father's desires. He was a murderer from the beginning and has nothing to do with the truth . . ." (8.43–44a).

The second important observation in the analysis of the Johannine attitude towards the Jews is the excommunication of the Johannine church from the synagogue through a formal ban, as we can see in chapter 9. The parents of the man born blind but healed by Jesus are afraid to enter into discussion of the healing with the Pharisees because ". . . they feared the Jews, for the Jews had already agreed that if anyone should confess him (Jesus) to be the Christ, (that one) was to be put out of the synagogue" (9.22). And indeed the final verdict on the man who was healed by Jesus is that ". . . they cast him out" (9.34).

A third key to understanding the Johannine portrait of the Jews is to realize that John sees the church as the replacement for Judaism in the world. Judaism itself is now an outmoded and illegitimate religion; its major interpretative symbols are no longer its own but belong to the church. This is the point of the great "I am" discourses (6.35; 8.12; 10.7; 10.14; 11.25; 14.6; 15.1). The Johannine church is now the only true people of God in the world, and to it belong the symbols of the life-world of Judaism.

The replacement motif begins in the famous prologue (1.1–18). John 1.1 echoes Genesis 1.1 but adds to the text of Genesis the important supplement of the presence of the pre-existent Christ (the Word) at the time of creation. The Word (who is the Lord of the church) is the real agency through whom the world was made. This is a subtle but intensely polemical emphasis. The darkness, the power opposed to God, has not been able to overcome God even in the crucifixion of Jesus. The light, a primary Jewish symbol, is here ascribed only to the church (1.5, 9). When the Jews rejected him, they forfeited their claim to be the people of God, for ". . . to all who received him, who believed in his name (i.e. all who are in the church), he gave power to become children of God" (1.11–12). The law, a second-rate revelation, came through Moses to the Jews, but grace and truth came through Jesus Christ (1.17). Did Moses, or any other Jew, see God? Certainly not! Jesus alone has seen God (1.18).

Open conflict between Jesus and Jews begins almost immediately (2.13–21). Jesus enters the temple and thrashes the merchants and moneychangers because they have perverted the purpose of the temple.

On the one hand the signs of Jesus depict the wonderful effect of the presence of Jesus. On the other hand, many of them are critical of Judaism. For instance, in the first sign (2.1–11) Judaism is like the water of purification; the church is the best wine saved until the last. Some scholars detect in the wine a reference to the eucharist, a rite much superior to the simple, outmoded rites of purification. Other signs are likewise anti-Jewish. The third (5.1–41), the fifth (6.1–15, 22–71) and the sixth (9.1–10.19) signs become the occasion for bitter exchanges between Jesus and the Jews in which his absolute superiority over them is demonstrated. In the last sign (11.1–57) the Jews are the victims of death, whereas Jesus alone is the source of life.

John 3.16, perhaps the verse most loved by Christians from the literature of the early church, is plainly anti-Jewish. This is especially clear when seen in its larger (3.1–21) and immediate (3.16–21) literary settings. Only those who believe in Jesus have eternal life. All others, including the Jews, are condemned. Even a *Samaritan woman* receives a better evaluation than the Jews (4.1–42).

John's skill as a writer reaches its peak in the arrest, trial and crucifixion of Jesus. Johannine irony is at its most penetrating here: things are just the opposite of what they seem. The Jews, in collusion with Pilate, seem to be in control, but the reader recognizes that the Johannine Jesus is really in control. For Jesus has already plainly said, "I have power to lay it (i.e. my life) down, and I have power to take it up again . . ." (10.18). So, to cite just one example, the reader is not surprised that the Jews attempt to question Jesus but are in fact questioned by him (18.19–24). The same pattern appears in the brief inquisition before Pilate (18.33–38).

John is clear that the Jews did not have the legal authority to put Jesus (or anyone else) to death (18.31). But the Jews are the moving force which leads Pilate to execute Jesus. They present Jesus as an evildoer (18.30) when they insist on the release of Barabbas (18.40) and when they continue to press for his death (19.1–15). The Johannine Pilate comes off as a nearly incompetent administrator who is manipulated by *the Jews who finally confess*, "We have no king but Caesar" (19.15)! The irony, of course, is that Pilate asks the right question, "Shall I crucify your King?" (18.15), and against the objection of the chief priests permits that title to hang ironically on the cross (19.21–22). The Jews have been responsible for the death of the one whom God sent for their own salvation and for the salvation of the world.

Hebrews: Christianity superior to Judaism

Hebrews is one of the most enigmatic documents written by the early church. It indicates neither its author nor the location of the community to whom it was written. In form it may be an early Christian homily, but on this, as on many matters related to its interpretation, scholars are widely disagreed. However, there can be no disagreement on its claim that Christianity is a superior religion to Judaism. Christianity alone can lead the believer to perfection.

Even the casual and uninformed reader quickly deduces that a knowledge of Judaism is required to understand the complexities of the text of Hebrews. Yet the Judaism which is presupposed by the writer is a Hellenistic Judaism, perhaps best exemplified in the writings of the learned Jew Philo of Alexandria (Dey, 1975).

When the reader grasps the world-view of Hebrews, the whole of the document, including its anti-Judaism, becomes plain. The world-view of the homily is much like that of the Fourth Gospel, although the vocabulary used by Hebrews to name and describe the parts of the world-view is different from that found in the Gospel of John.

In Hebrews, the universe is presented as consisting of two

realms: the realm of heaven and the realm of the earth. Heaven is a place of perfection, which in this sermon refers to immediate access to God. To be perfected is to be in the full, immediate presence of God. The earth is a realm of imperfection in which access to God is partial and available only through intermediaries.

In this theological system, one of the major images for Jesus is that of pioneer and perfecter of the believers. Jesus has come down from the heavenly realm and has been perfected through suffering. Therefore he is able to lead many human beings to glory, i.e. to perfection (2.10; 5.9; 7.28). Perfection is the goal of the Christian life (10.14; 11.40; 12.3, 22–23) and is not possible through the law (7.19; 9.9; 10.1) but is possible only through Jesus.

One of the writer's literary techniques is to use many different names to speak of the same realities. The following chart sets out some representative designations and qualities of the two spheres. Note how many of the earthly (imperfect) realities are identified with Judaism.

HEAVENLY REALITIES

(perfection)

Salvation (1.4; 2.3, 10; 5.9; 9.28); rest (3.11, 18; 4.1–11); heaven (4.4; 8.1; 9.23, 24); things eternal (5.9); Spirit (9.14); inheritance (9.15); the true tent (8.2; 9.11); heavenly things (8.5, 9.23); better covenant (8.6, 8); new covenant (8.8, 13; 10.16; 12.24), not made with hands (9.11); a better country (10.34; 11.16); things not seen (11.1); will not see death (11.5); city which has foundations (11.10, 16); things to come (11.20); heavenly Jerusalem (12.22); better things (12.24); things that cannot be shaken (12.27); outside the camp (13.11, 13) everlasting covenant (13.20).

EARTHLY REALITIES

(imperfection)

Partaking of flesh and blood (2.14); suffering (2.18; 11.25; 13.3); bondage (2.15); eternal judgment (6.2); earth (8.4;

11.13); shadow of heavenly things (8.5); first tent (9.2–8); made with hands (9.25); things which are seen (11.1); strangers and pilgrims (11.13); illegitimate children (12.8); death (12.9–15); bondage (12.15); things which are made (12.27); in the body (13.3); tent (13.10); no lasting city (13.14); Egypt (3.16; 8.9; 11.26–27)

Jesus descends from the heavenly realm, is perfected through suffering, and is able to open the way for many others who follow in his path to be perfected. He alone makes it possible to come to God.

The structure of Hebrews is itself anti-Jewish. After a brief introduction of Jesus (1.1–4), the main part of the letter is a series of comparisons in which the author demonstrates the superiority of Jesus over the angels (1.5–2.18), over Moses (3.1–4.13), over the high priest (4.14–6.20), over Melchizedek (7.1–28), over the worship of Judaism (8.1–10.18). In 10.19–11.40 the author shows that while many Jewish heroes and heroines had faith, they did not have the faith that gets them perfected. 12.1–13.19 pictures the life of the true believer, a life which is often contrasted with the life of the Jews (e.g. 12.18–24).

According to Hebrews, the figures and religious system with whom Jesus is compared are only intermediaries. They do not provide false information about God, but the information they do provide is incomplete and does not lead to perfection. Jews themselves are not vilified as such in the way that they are in the Gospel tradition. But in a direct and forceful way Hebrews claims that Judaism is a second-rate religion.

Conclusion

None of the other documents in the canonical literature of the early church deals as prominently with Jewish themes as do the materials we have examined. Nor are the anti-Jewish elements as systematic or as extensive as in the Gospels, Acts and Hebrews.

A review of this kind can leave the impression that the

writings of the early church are only, or at least primarily, anti-Jewish. In closing, perhaps it is helpful to remember that we have brought anti-Jewish elements to the surface in order to see them clearly. While the origins of such themes are understandable in the light of the situation of the early church, those days are long gone. The gospel itself compels us to criticize these texts so that justice may be done to the Jewish community, and so that our interpretation of the texts does not deny the promise of the love of God to each and all.

— 4 —

Interpreting Difficult Texts

Introduction

We have looked at anti-Judaism as a way of interpreting both the Christian faith and scriptural texts. We have surveyed its use in the history of preaching, and seen how it worked its way into the Gospels, Acts and Hebrews – those canonical materials produced in the conflictual situation of the latter third of the first century.

Now we turn our attention to the question of what preachers are to do with these texts. This issue cannot be avoided because, problematic as a given pericope might be in any number of ways, nonetheless it will probably turn up in the lectionary and be read publicly in services of worship. Also, the same text will be read privately by lay people who study the scriptures or contemplate them devotionally. Troublesome texts have a life and influence of their own and therefore cannot responsibly be ignored. Preachers must deal with them. Accordingly we offer the following reflections on ways of doing so.

Alternatives no longer available

1. Creating a private canon

In the eighteenth century, Thomas Jefferson spent his leisure time while President of the United States on the task of editing the Gospels. He cut out the parts that were unintelligible to an Enlightenment mentality and what remained – the moral teachings of Jesus – was a considerably slimmed-down version.

Jefferson's result was his own canon of scripture, not that of any community.

We have all known preachers who in effect created their own, sometimes highly idiosyncratic, canons. One whom I remember hardly ever preached on any biblical text other than the Letter of James. The temptation simply to preach on passages with which we are comfortable must be resisted, not least because it relieves us of any serious wrestling with scripture, thereby denying us the possibility of a growing and deepening under-standing of scripture itself. Another reason for not ducking awkward passages is that these passages, in their diversity, reflect diverse communities in the early church, with diverse experiences, which may help us to speak to the diversity of the contemporary world and church. It is impoverishing to the heart and mind to work with a slim canon.

Besides, if we today were to eliminate as unworthy of attention all passages that are in any way offensive, we might well wind up with little left. The main problem with this approach is that we deceive ourselves by using it. Not only do texts have a life of their own. Other preachers, not bothered by the difficulties a text poses, will go ahead and expound it. Some – not all – television ministers and celebrity clergy will uncritically proclaim anything and everything as the absolute truth. Theirs should not be the only voices heard by Christians. If the only preachers who deal with the texts in which there are negative images of Jews and Judaism are the ones who reinforce such images in the minds of their parishioners, no countervailing voice will be heard in the church. Anti-Judaism will continue to thrive and the church will persist in sowing the seeds of popular antisemitism. Therefore it is morally incumbent on the rest of us to learn to deal critically with such texts.

2. Refusing to budge

At the other pole one finds those preachers who may well be appalled at the history of the church's "teaching of contempt" for Jews and Judaism, yet who remain rocklike in their commit-ment to biblical inerrancy. However much they deplore the fact that down through the millennia people have poured into

certain texts accumulated prejudice and hostility, to the neglect
of their meaning, they still refuse to admit that any distortion
crept into the scriptures

Thus when John has Jesus say that "the Jews' " father is
"the devil, and your will is to do your father's desires", and
goes on to claim that their father was a murderer and liar
from the beginning (John 8.44), the unbudging supporter of
inerrancy is confident that the mind of Jesus Christ is accurately
portrayed in this passage. Hence the claim made by the passage
cannot be questioned. To do so would be to challenge Christ
himself. Because inerrancy asserts an *identity* between what God
wants to communicate to us and what comes to expression in
the scriptures, it removes the distinction between the text and
God, thus putting the text above criticism. The word for this
is "bibliolatry". Consequently, holding to the inerrancy of
scripture is as closed an option for us as is the willingness to
disregard its authority by selecting only the parts with which
we are comfortable. To exercize either option is to allow anti-
Judaism to continue to thrive unabated.

A digression into inerrancy

Readers who are troubled by the above discussion or who in
spite of some misgivings may still feel a tug on the heartstrings
from the doctrine of inerrancy might benefit from a brief
consideration of the history of the idea. Where did it come from
and what does it mean? Why does it, where it is believed,
support the view that the church displaced Israel in the covenant
with God?

To answer these questions, we will summarize some of the
main points in an excellent essay on the subject, whose authors
(Edward Farley and Peter C. Hodgson) refer to it as "the
scripture principle". The doctrine was initiated among Jews in
the Diaspora following the Babylonian exile. No longer having
the land, temple or priesthood they created in their place the
synagogue and the written Torah (Farley and Hodgson: 63).
Although the scripture principle represented a significant
development in Israelite religion, it was not free from ambiguity.

With it the idea of scripture came to involve a written deposit of definitive revelation that functioned to authorize cultic and moral regulations. It exhaustively locates revelation in the past and claims that the text "is totally and equally valid in all its parts and details" (Farley and Hodgson: 63).

In spite of the church's claim that there had been a new revelation, it adopted the scripture principle with its denial of this very claim. Therefore Christianity's embrace of the scripture principle meant that salvation history had to be divided into new periods (Farley and Hodgson: 65) and the content of scripture had to shift. In this way, the Old Testament was accorded only provisional validity while the New Testament became scripture in the definitive sense, thus producing a hyphenated scripture of two Testaments. The genre of scripture shifted from *Torah* to gospel. Supersessionism is built into the scripture principle. All of this is self-contradictory, of course, since either there can or cannot be new revelation and either scripture is or is not immutable.

Yet with these modifications, the assertions of the scripture principle were retained. Included among these are that the text of scripture and its content possess the "qualities of inerrancy, infallibility, and absolute truthfulness . . ." (Farley and Hodgson: 66), that the contents of the text are *level*, the inerrant truth being distributed evenly throughout, and that this truth is *immutably* valid for all future generations. If scripture is inerrant, infallible and absolutely true, there can be no theological criticism of scripture, no conversation with it about matters of mutual concern. All one may do with scripture is to cite and translate it for the present; critical inquiry is out of bounds.

Although created by exilic Judaism, the scripture principle and its doctrines of inerrancy and immutability were overcome in Judaism by the Pharisees. They laid the Oral Torah alongside the written Torah and developed an exegetical method ("you have read, but the meaning is") which allowed them to revolutionize the would-be immutable meanings deposited in the text (Rivkin, 1978: 209–311). Matthew's Gospel frequently depicts Jesus as practising a method like that of the Pharisees ("You have heard, but I say unto you").

Because the division of salvation history into new periods in the Christian form of the scripture-principle builds the displacement ideology into the very meaning of scripture itself, the claim that the church superseded Judaism is part and parcel of what inerrancy has come to mean. This is one reason why such a view of the text leaves one unable to move, even after having become aware of the teaching of contempt for Jews and its pay-off in Hitler's systematic programme of the elimination of all Jews. Moreover the claims that the text and its content are immutable, inerrant and absolutely true prohibit the application to it of all forms of the hermeneutic of suspicion, including ideology critique, and indeed of any authentically prophetic questioning of received meanings.

Today scholars who call themselves "evangelical" will often seek inconsistently to shore up their commitments to inerrancy by using such conservative results of historical criticism as fit their views (e.g., Glasser: 68, who uses J. A. T. Robinson's dating of the Gospels to argue for their infallibility). The result incoherently blends inerrancy with the use of the historical-critical method, not recognizing that such a method, regardless of its results, cannot get beyond probabilities to absolute truth on historical matters (Tillich: 227). Using a probabilistic method to support an absolutist position is an odd way of doing one's theological business.

Promising options

1. The gospel is the key to the scriptures

To find constructive alternative ways to interpret difficult texts, we begin with Luther's understanding of the word of God. We have already cited Luther, unfavourably, in the history of anti-Jewish preaching. What we are about to consider is Luther's own deeper insight, which *should* have led him to avoid anti-Judaism, and from which we can benefit greatly. Luther's anti-Judaism is to be rejected for reasons that Luther himself provides.

Among many contemporary Protestants, Luther's approach

to scripture is a forgotten alternative. By the "word of God", Luther means several things: the second person of the Trinity, God's power manifest in the creation of all things, the incarnate Lord, the scriptures which witness to the word, and the pro- clamation (preaching) through which the word is heard by believers. We will concentrate on the relation of the scriptures to the word of God.

For Luther, we know the word of God through the event of Jesus Christ. The purpose of the scriptures is not to add to the word of God, "for this much is beyond question, that all the Scriptures point to Christ alone" (*Luther's Works*, 35: 132). Christ is presented to us as the gospel, the good news, and when Luther discusses the relation of scripture to tradition he is not contending strictly for the primacy of scripture but for the primacy of the gospel to which scripture testifies: "The Scrip- tures must be understood in favour of Christ, not against him. For that reason they must either refer to him or must not be held to be true Scriptures" (*Luther's Works*, 34: 112). Indeed the most appropriate form of the gospel is not in writing at all, but in its lively spoken proclamation. Scripture's authority lies not in the canon, but in the gospel that is found in the canon and is the measure of its interpretation. In asserting that the Bible must be its own interpreter, Luther does not merely intend that we should compare texts but states that the central message of the Bible, the gospel, is the *sole* key to understanding it. Here is Luther's explicit comment on how his view of biblical interpretation bears on our topic:

> . . . it is not enough or in any sense Christian to preach the works, life, and words of Christ as historical facts, as if the knowledge of these would suffice for the conduct of life; yet this is the fashion among those who must today be regarded as our best preachers. Far less is it sufficient to say nothing at all about Christ and to teach instead the laws of men and the decrees of the fathers. Now there are not a few who preach Christ and read about him that they may move men's affections to sympathy with Christ, to anger against the Jews, and such childish . . . nonsense. Rather ought Christ to be

preached to the end that faith in him may be established that
he may not only be Christ, but be Christ for you and me . . .
(Luther, 1961: 65–6).

A recent writer puts it this way: "Exposition of a text does not
assure the preaching of a message that will build up persons in
the faith" (Williams: 3). We are obliged, he affirms, to "preach
the gospel. In some cases, this may mean preaching *to* a text,
rather than *from* a text. To preach to a text is to bring the gospel
to bear on a text that does not contain the gospel" (Williams:
3). The words of scripture must serve the word of God, not *vice
versa*.

What do we learn from Luther? We discover that it is the
good news (of God's love graciously offered to each and all and
therefore of God's command that justice be done to each and
all) that we are given to preach. Texts and interpretations that
contradict this good news are inappropriate and to be excluded.
We are to preach the *one* word of God's good news, and not the
many words of the text. We are not to preach the "facts" of the
life of Jesus so as to move people to anger against Jews, but the
good news of God's gracious disposition toward us, made known
to us in Jesus Christ. On occasion, we may have to preach *to* or
even *against* the text. We are free to do so, even obligated to do
so, provided we responsibly proclaim the gospel.

2. Scripture shapes identity

Of several recent proposals for dealing with the scriptures, we
turn to David Kelsey's suggestion that the biblical writings
supply the images, concepts, parables, etc., that "evoke, nur-
ture, and correct the dispositions, beliefs, policies, emotions,
etc., that are basic to the identities of members of the community
and to the identity of the community itself" (Kelsey: 51). Texts
used in these ways function to create new personal identities.

For the problem with which we are dealing, that of overcom-
ing the anti-Judaism found both in texts and their interpretation, Kelsey's proposal may be viewed as having two poles,
one empirical and descriptive, and the other normative and
prescriptive.

The descriptive aspect of Kelsey's suggestion points out that, in fact, the use of scripture in the church functions to shape the identity of members of the community and of the community as a whole. Biblical writings in fact operate and have operated in the church to shape identity. They are used to shape attitudes towards the neighbour, to reflect on our faith, and to regulate our behaviour.

Anti-Judaism in the scriptures and in their interpretation from the pulpit has done precisely this: it has shaped Christian identity by telling us who we are. It has said that we are not Jewish, that we are anti-Jewish, that we are better than Jewish, that we as a new spiritual people have replaced the old carnal Jews, that we are ruled by grace, not law, and so forth. It has shaped attitudes towards the contemporary Jewish neighbour in ways that are either negative or reflect blissful neglect of that neighbour's situation. It has shaped behaviour towards Jews either by creating attitudes that result in hostile action or by conveying the impression that the only way to love our Jewish neighbours is by working to convert them away from being Jewish.

Thus Kelsey's proposal that scripture shapes identity functions descriptively to remind all of us who preach of the seriousness of what we do. More than we realize, we help to shape the character of people. If we fail to attend to the way in which we do this, we may do it in extremely negative ways. Empirically, therefore, the fact is that scriptures as interpreted in church shape identity. How they do so is incredibly important.

So Kelsey suggests a norm or test by which preachers can decide how to interpret, set forth and teach the varied meanings of scripture and allow them to play their various roles in addressing beliefs, feelings and attitudes. This norm, as Kelsey defines it, "is the actuality of the inauguration in and for the world of the eschatological rule of God in the resurrection of the crucified Jesus" (Kelsey: 58).

The disquiet which we have with Kelsey's proposal is his claim that God's eschatological rule over history *began* with the resurrection of Jesus. If we take the story of Jesus in the context of the whole biblical narrative, should we not say that God's eschatological reign begins with the story of the creation itself? Does not God rule over that which God has made? Is not this rule announced in the story of the Exodus, with the question whether it is God or Pharaoh who is in charge? How could Jesus' first followers – all of whom were Jews – have recognized the rule of God had they absolutely no prior experience of it? We raise this issue lest Kelsey's way of formulating his norm be taken as another form of the old promise/fulfilment dichotomy.

Thus we would want to modify Kelsey's formulation, to claim that in Jesus Christ the Gentile church learns of God's eschatological rule over history and that faith in Jesus Christ is not a substitute or replacement for Israel's faith but a new wider awareness of God's presence. Thus revised, Kelsey's norm will prove helpful to preachers in dealing with difficult texts.

To live in response to God's eschatological rule is to be open to the possibility ever offered us anew as God graciously and commandingly calls us forward to that future which lies ahead of Christians as well as of Jews. To live eschatologically is to live forward. To live forward entails, among other things, envisioning a new future for relations between Christians and Jews. God calls us forward from the sinfulness and narrowness of the past to the abundance of life that can only be had by responding in trust to what God gives and calls us to become, people who live in love and justice with all their neighbours in the house that we call "earth". When, therefore, we find the very hostility and narrowness away from which God is calling us embedded in texts of scripture, we are to interpret those texts in the light of God's eschatological rule announced to us in Jesus Christ.

3. Scripture re-presents God's grace

Another contemporary proposal for dealing with the scriptures, one that gathers to itself Luther's central insight and complements Kelsey's, is made by Schubert M. Ogden, who draws an analogy between the authority of scripture and the authority of a judge in a courtroom. The judge has considerable authority over the defendant, yet the judge must arrive at judgments that are in accord with the law. The law which governs the defendant also governs the judge, so that if the judge rules capriciously the defendant may appeal over the judge's head to a higher court. Here, Ogden refers to Luther's claim that Jesus Christ is "King of scripture" (*Rex scripturae*) and that we may appeal beyond scripture to Christ and his gospel. Scripture "itself ultimately stands on the same level as those who are subject to its authority *vis-à-vis* Jesus the Christ" (Ogden, 1976: 246). Scripture is authoritative, but not authoritarian, and its authority is limited to matters of appropriateness, since issues of intelligibility and morality must be worked out afresh in every new historical situation.

Because the authority of scripture derives from Jesus Christ, being subject to him and his gospel, then nothing in scripture is authoritative unless it is authorized by Christ "through the church's continuing experience under the guidance of the Holy Spirit" (Ogden, 1976: 250). The canonical texts which the early church produced are criticizable Christian witness. Merely to show that an assertion is found in them fails to authorize it as theologically appropriate. To do that one would have to give reasons why this witness "is itself authorized by the apostolic witness of faith" (Ogden, 1976: 257).

The strength of Ogden's proposal for our task lies in its total avoidance of the works-righteousness inherent in all forms of the displacement ideology. The "new" knowledge of God on which Christians can lay hold is identical with the primordial revelation of God previously re-presented in the faith of Israel. Our salvation (saving, transforming knowledge of God and of ourselves) does not "become possible" in Christ – a statement that is nowhere made in the apostolic writings – but in him what was always possible now "becomes manifest" (Ogden, 1961: 143). This statement reflects a radical acceptance of the Reformation principle "by grace alone": when "the event of Jesus becomes a condition apart from which God is not free to be a gracious God, the heretical doctrine of works-righteousness achieves its final and most dangerous triumph" (Ogden, 1961: 145).

Ogden's understanding of how scripture is to be interpreted

renders explicit the theocentric basis of the Christian witness –
that "we are Christ's", but that "Christ is God's" (I Cor. 3.23;
11.3). Also it makes the only condition of salvation one that can
be formulated without reference to Jesus Christ, as stated in
the parable of the Last Judgment (Matt. 25.31–46). The only
demand that we must meet to receive salvation is that we accept
God's love for ourselves and thereby become liberated to
respond to the concrete needs of the neighbour (Ogden, 1961:
144).

What do we learn from Ogden about handling difficult texts?
First, we learn that we may have a genuine conversation with
those texts about the meaning of the Christian faith. The texts,
no less than we, are under the critique of the gospel, and their
authority is that of a conversation partner with whom we must
deal, as in any authentic conversation, respectfully. We also
learn that the text, so to speak, must deal respectfully with us;
that is, that the text may not lord it over us because the text is
not the Lord. Second, we learn that the gospel of God's love
freely offered to each and all and of God's justice therefore
commanded to be done to each and all is the norm of appropriateness for measuring each text.

Third, we learn that the gospel of God's absolutely free grace
prohibits us from making anything – even the acceptance of
Jesus Christ – a condition apart from which God is not free to
be gracious. The deepest error of works-righteousness is to turn
a gift into a condition. Fourth, we learn that salvation became
manifest, not possible, in Jesus Christ. It had already been
possible, indeed always, but not yet to us. The revelatory event
is always an "already, but not yet". Paul the apostle, who was
one of our best theologians in these matters, declared that in
Jesus Christ God's promises to the patriarchs found confirm-
ation (Romans 15.8). He never says that they found "fulfilment" there, nor that they first became possible there. To make
either of these statements would be to set a condition on God's
grace.

4. Observing the hermeneutical axioms of scripture

The suggestion offered by canonical criticism is that we look at the scriptures as distillates from a living tradition, something on the following order. At any point on its path through history, we find the people Israel confronted with a hermeneutical task. They have a tradition and the new experience of the contemporary generation. In order to understand the new experience they must interpret it in the light of their tradition. By doing so, they incorporate it into the tradition. But at the same time they must reinterpret the tradition if it is to include the new experience and to be credible in face of it. They must do both if they are to pass on their faith to the next generation. "Process," as James Sanders says, "was there from the start and continues unabated through and after the periods of intense canonical process of stabilization" (Sanders, 1984: 31).

Every time Israel interprets its faith it interprets it again. We never find it simply living among uninterpreted experience. Indeed, as Alfred North Whitehead once remarked: "If we desire a record of uninterpreted experience, we must ask a stone to record its autobiography" (Whitehead: 15). In re-interpreting its tradition, Israel sometimes found it necessary to reject prior interpretations: "As I live, says the Lord God, this proverb shall no more be used by you in Israel" (Ezekiel 18.2).

Over time, therefore, Israel offered many accounts of its self-understanding. To find the key that unlocks the scriptures, canonical criticism suggests that we attend to Israel's her-meneutical principles, the axioms in the light of which it characteristically reinterpreted its tradition. This will provide a clue today as to how scripture is appropriately understood. The pertinence of canonical criticism to the task of removing anti-Judaism from preaching is clear from this remark: "Christianity has become so systematically Marcionite and anti-Semitic that only a truly radical revival of the concept of canon as applied to the Bible will, I think, counter it" (Sanders, 1984: xv).

The context in which the hermeneutical axioms of scripture are set is theocentric. That is, the first point to note is that the

Bible is a monotheizing literature; it regularly struggles "within and against polytheistic contexts to affirm God's oneness" (Sanders, 1984: 52). An interpretation of any given text, then, to be appropriate, would have to remember the oneness of God. Doing so would help preachers steer clear of a Marcionite interpretation in all its forms and to avoid claims that imply a duplicity in God, that God provided a "better" revelation or religion to the church than to Israel. Such claims deny the faithfulness and trustworthiness of God and implicitly raise the question why *we* should trust God.

Within this theocentric context, Sanders labels the first hermeneutical axiom as "constitutive". This axiom stresses that God loves *this particular community*. It reminds the community (or the individual) that "God loves *you*". It comforts the community, reassures it and edifies it. That is, it builds up or constitutes this community of faith.

The second of Israel's hermeneutical axioms is termed the "prophetic". It stresses that God is the God *of all*, not merely of this particular community. God does not just love Israel; God also loves the Egyptians, the Persians and the Romans. For example, to remind a group of British or American Christians today that God loves the inhabitants of the Soviet Union calls those so reminded to a fresh attitude towards some of their global neighbours.

Each axiom – the one that constitutes the community and the one that challenges it – gives voice to the grace of God. In situations that require it, the prophetic mode is stressed and Israel is reminded of God's love for Egypt and Assyria (Isaiah 19.25). In others the constitutive mode is accented and Israel is reminded that she is the first among God's beloved.

The two axioms are equally important and require one another. Merely to use the constitutive axiom is to commit two sins: exclusivism and idolatry. The constitutive axiom, if divorced from the prophetic, affirms that God loves only us and that to be loved by God others must join us. To read the scriptures in a merely constitutive way "can issue in a totally denominational, if not tribal, reading of the whole Bible" (Sanders, 1984: 66). Such an exclusivist reading denies to God the freedom to be gracious apart from Jesus Christ, thereby turning God's gift of Christ into a condition apart from which God is not free to be gracious.

On the other hand, merely to use the prophetic axiom to state the meaning of faith today, forgetting the constitutive, would be equally malicious. Constantly to berate a congregation with a sense of its own sinfulness and lack of concern for justice, while reminding it that God loves everyone else, leaves it without the sense of God's grace that builds it up and enables it to act justly towards neighbours. If the error of a cliquish use of the constitutive axiom is exclusivism, the error of an incessant strumming of the prophetic theme is emptiness. The congregation will feel abandoned by God. Therefore the constitutive and prophetic axioms must be used together in a dialectical relationship.

With regard to Jews and Gentiles, we find Paul the apostle using both axioms within the context of a theocentric emphasis on the oneness of God: "For we hold that a man is justified by faith apart from works of law. Or is God the God of Jews only? Is he not the God of Gentiles also? Yes, of Gentiles also, since God is one; and he will justify the circumcised on the ground of their faith and the uncircumcised through their faith. Do we then overthrow the law by this faith? By no means! On the contrary, we uphold the law" (Romans 3.28–31). Like Paul, preachers today should pursue a theocentric hermeneutic as they pass on the tradition to their congregations.

Canonical criticism is a contemporary, scholarly way of restating Luther's use of the gospel of God's free grace as the key to the scriptures. God's love is graciously offered to all, and to us. What Ogden calls the gospel or the earliest apostolic witness – the good news of God's love offered freely to each and all and the command that justice be done to each and all because God loves them – is another way of stating what Sanders discerns as the hermeneutical axioms found in scripture. These three proposals for interpreting scripture are not alternatives to one another, nor are preachers being asked to choose among them. The gospel is inclusive because it is gracious – if even we are accepted by God, are not the Jews as well? Luther, Ogden and Sanders substantially agree as to what constitutes an appropriate interpretation of scripture, and Kelsey's way of stating the norm reminds us that God, who is God of the future as well as of the present and past, is not yet finished with Jews, Christians and their relationship to each other.

What do preachers learn from canonical criticism? They realize that every time they step into the pulpit or classroom they are teaching the Christian faith, interpreting it anew for people, including themselves, who have never before been in this situation. When we interpret the Christian faith we engage in an act of tradition, as the Latin root of the word (*traditio*=to pass on) tells us. What makes the act of reinterpreting and handing down tradition authentic is attention to the critical standards in the light of which we devise our reinterpretations. Canonical criticism suggests that those standards are a theo-centric emphasis on the oneness of God coupled with the dipolar awareness that God's love is unqualifiedly all-inclusive, including others and us and commanding justice for them as for us.

5. *Not being "blind-sided" by ideology*

In football, a player looking in one direction frequently has the experience of being blocked out of the flow of the play by a player attacking from another direction. This is called being "blind-sided". Sometimes it happens to all of us that when we are trying our best to interpret the Christian faith we are blind-sided by ideology.

As we have tried to show, there is a strong anti-Jewish animus in the texts of scripture and in the history of preaching. This ideology, until we become conscious and critical of it, is also in us and makes us vulnerable to traditional and scriptural anti-Judaism. When we say that anti-Judaism is in us, we do not mean that Christians are consciously and intentionally anti-Jewish, purposely spread anti-Jewish prejudice, and the like.

Rather, anti-Judaism is very much like sexism. That is, it is a way of using language to define oneself and others, a way of using language that creates and reinforces social attitudes and realities, and a way of using language of which the users are unaware until it is brought to their attention. Like sexism, anti-Judaism is also a tradition, i.e., in the sense that we inherit it and pass it on, and the truth seems to be that we are highly determined by traditions of which we are unaware. We are often blind-sided by anti-Judaism because it has not only shaped our attitudes, but by shaping them makes us accept unquestioningly the anti-Judaism that then turns up in, e.g., texts of scripture. What can help us avoid being blind-sided in this way?

For at least a partial answer to this question, we turn to one last suggestion for interpreting scripture, one that goes by the name "ideology criticism". Ideology criticism is a way of taking steps to correct points of view and attitudes found in scripture, tradition and ourselves when those attitudes serve the desolation of life and the subjugation of human beings.

Because at its core biblical faith stands for the redemption of life from enslavement and exploitation, a story of redemption that begins at least with the Exodus, biblical faith itself requires that ideology be removed from the re-presentations of faith offered by preachers. Because the religious negation of Jewish existence has led to contempt, injustice and, however circuitously, genocide, anti-Judaism stands condemned by the biblical principle of the redemption of human life.

Ideology criticism is a way of making ourselves aware that truth is disfigured by social interest:

It is claimed that every group, every nation, every religious community produces – by a largely unconscious process – a perception of reality expressed in special dogmas that promotes its own interest, defends the group against others and makes it easier for the rulers to exercise their power. From the beginning, the Church preached the Christian message with an anti-Jewish ideology. When, in later centuries, the Church gained political influence and social power, the anti-Jewish ideology translated itself into social structures that excluded the Jews, with the result that the Christian gospel came to promote the oppression of a living people (Baum: 141).

Because such treatment of human beings contradicts the gospel's promise of God's love to each and all and of God's command that justice be done to each and all, such ideological disfigurements of the Christian spirit should be eliminated no matter where we find them. That sexist ideology, e.g., is found in scripture is now widely accepted, as is the understanding that sexism is not the gospel and that Christians should not preach it. Being aware that anti-Judaism is a disfigurement of the gospel by social interests frees and requires us to remove it from preaching and replace it with a genuine concern for love and justice.

Conclusion

In the first chapter, we gave three reasons why anti-Judaism should be excised from Christian preaching, arguing that it is inappropriate to the gospel, unintelligible and immoral. Here we have provided a series of hermeneutical strategies, all of which converge on the same conclusion, indicating not only *that* anti-Judaism should be removed from our preaching, but *how* scripture can be interpreted in order to do that. If preachers remember nothing else from this chapter, it is hoped that they will always remind themselves to ask three questions of their interpretations of texts of scripture. Is this appropriate to the gospel of God's absolutely unconditional love? Is this intelligible? Is this moral, does it promote justice for Jews and, by implication, for all minority groups?

— 5 —

Case Studies in Selected Texts

Introduction

When ministers prepare to preach from a text from the canonical literature of the early church which contains anti-Judaism, what should they do? In this chapter, we outline concerns to be taken into account in exegesis, consider representative texts and suggest possible directions for sermons on the texts.

Two significant assessments need to be made concerning any text in which Jewish motifs or characters appear. The first is the identification of the tone and attitude of the reference(s) towards things Jewish. One may ask a simple question of every text in which Jewish elements are found. "What is the tone and attitude of the reference?"

The second is the assessment of the appropriateness of the text in the light of the gospel. Is the attitude towards the Jews in the text consistent with the promise of the love of God for each and all and the command that justice be done to each and all? When the content of the text is not appropriate to the gospel, then the vocation of the preacher is to tell the truth about the text. As mentioned in the previous chapter, the pastor must sometimes preach against the text. Yet is is not enough for the sermon to dismantle the text; the calling of the Christian preacher is to announce the good news of God's redeeming presence. Therefore even in a sermon which tells the truth about the bad news found in the text, the preacher will want to proclaim the good news which is the heart of the gospel itself.

In the canonical literature written by the early church,

we may distinguish three distinct attitudes toward Jews and Judaism. 1. Some texts contain good news for both Christians and for Jews. These passages should be proclaimed forcefully from Christian pulpits. 2. Other texts, primarily from the Pauline corpus, have been misunderstood by Christian interpreters with the result that they are seen as presenting Judaism in a negative light. Many such texts are now recognized as putting forth a strong and positive meaning. In these cases, the work of the preacher is to reinterpret the texts so as to cast their true light across the congregation. 3. Many texts present good news for Christians at the expense of bad news for Jews. Such texts require theological correction from the pulpit.

Examples of each of the three main types of texts are discussed in the following exegeses. For the sake of brevity and clarity, we have focused attention on matters related to Judaism and have not considered other aspects of the texts. To be specific, we have chosen texts included in the Common Lectionary in use in the United States; where this lectionary is not used, it should nevertheless be possible to apply the approach to other similar texts.

Texts of good news

Ephesians 2.11–22 (the Ninth Sunday after Pentecost in Year B) is a classic example of a text which gives a positive evaluation to the relationship between Judaism and Christianity. The text honours the distinctions between Judaism and Christianity and also affirms their mutuality of service to the one true and living God.

The text is addressed to Gentile Christians, as is clear from the opening words: "Therefore, remember that at one time *you Gentiles* in the flesh. . . ." Throughout the passage, the Gentiles are the only audience directly addressed.

The structure of the passage depicts the journey of the Gentiles from alienation from God and the Jewish community to fellowship with God and with the people who have earlier witnessed to God in the world. Ephesians 2.11–22 is written in the literary form of a chiasmus. In chiastic structure, the elements of a passage are placed in a reverse parallel order so that the parallel elements illuminate one another, as in this simple outline.

A
  B
  B'
A'

In such a chiasmus, the meaning of A is interpreted in A' (and *vice versa*) and the meaning of B is expanded in B' (and *vice versa*).

The passage before us is an antithetical chiasmus, which means that the parallel elements exist in contrasting relationship. Calvin L. Porter of Christian Theological Seminary, Indianapolis, has laid out the chiastic structure of the passage in Table 1. The corresponding words and phrases in the parallel elements are in italics. The Gentiles move from being alienated from Israel, without hope and without God, to reconciliation with God and with Israel. Because of the grace of God in Christ, the Gentile church can now be considered a holy temple in whom dwells the spirit of God. Note that the central concern of the text, in elements K and K', is the situation between Gentile Christians and Jews. By abolishing the law of condemnation, Christ has created a new relationship, characterized as "one new human being in place of two".

At no point in the passage does the author suggest the superiority of Gentile Christianity to Jewish life, nor does the passage claim that Jewish practices are obsolete. Rather, as Markus Barth says, "Ephesians affirms that now, since Messiah has come, and has made and proclaimed peace, God has revealed the will and the power not only to appear but to 'dwell' (2.22) among the Gentile-born Ephesians – without ceasing to be faithful to Israel" (Barth, 1974: 321; cf. Barth, 1959; 123–35).

In a sermon on this text, the preacher can specifically claim its remarks about the Gentile Christians as the story of the modern church. *We Gentiles* are descended from these Ephesians who were once far off, alienated from the commonwealth of Israel and strangers to the promises of God. Particularly helpful

Table One

Chiastic Structure of Ephesians 2.11–22

A ¹¹Therefore remember that at one time you Gentiles *in the flesh*

  B called the uncircumcision by what is called the circumcision, which is made *in the flesh by hands,*

    C ¹²remember that you were at that time *separated from Christ*

      D *alienated from the commonwealth of Israel*

        E and *strangers* to the covenants of promise,

          F having no hope and *without God* in the world.

            G ¹³But now in Christ Jesus you who were once *far off*

              H have been *brought near* in the blood of Christ.

                I ¹⁴For *he is our peace*, who has made us both one,

                  J and has broken down the dividing wall of *hostility,*

                    K by *abolishing in his flesh* the law of commandments and ordinances

                    K′ that he might *create in himself* one new (human being) in the place of the two

                  J so making *peace* ¹⁶ and might *reconcile* us both to God in one body through the cross.

                I′ thereby bringing the *hostility* to an end.

              H′ ¹⁷And he came and preached peace to you who were *far off*

            G′ and peace to *those* who were *near;*

          F ¹⁸for through *him* we both have access in one *Spirit* to the *Father*

        E ¹⁹So then you are no longer *strangers* and *sojourners,*

      D but you are *fellow citizens with the saints* and *members of the household of God,*

    C ²⁰built upon the foundation of the apostles and prophets, *Christ Jesus himself being the chief cornerstone,*

  B in whom the whole structure is joined together and grows into *a holy temple in the Lord;*

A′ in whom you also are built into it for a dwelling place of God *in the Spirit.*

to the homily would be identification of particular instances in "modern Gentile life" which show that life to be one of alienation and of being strangers to God. Only by grace have we come to know God, to discover peace and to find our place in the service of God alongside the Jewish community. In order to make the sermon concrete, the preacher may wish to point to specific things held in common by Jews and Christians and to specific ways in which the contemporary witness of the two communities points to the one God.

Texts in need of reinterpretation

We shall consider three examples of texts which need to be reinterpreted. The task of the preacher in these instances is to show that the common Christian understanding of the text is misleading and needs to be replaced by another line of thought which is more faithful to the meaning of the text.

A. *Galatians 3.23–29* is appointed to be read in Year C on the Fifth Sunday after Pentecost. The pericope is usually taken to rest on opposition between the law and the gospel (which is available only through Christian faith as opposed to the straitjacket of Jewish legalism). But in the light of the fresh understanding of the law in the first century (articulated above on p. 38), we shall see that this is not correct. Instead, the fundamental subject-matter of this passage is condemnation and promise as these pertain to Gentiles.

H.-D. Betz has won scholarly consensus with his argument that Galatians is an example of a Graeco-Roman "apologetic letter" (Betz, 1979: 14ff.). In the apologetic letter, the author defends a position by laying out the position and its defence in a standard format common to such letters.

According to Betz's analysis of the structure of the letter, the cause of the writing (called the *exordium*) is found in 1.6–9. The events which led to the writing of the letter (*narratio*) are described in 1.12–2.14. The main thesis of the letter (*propositio*) is set forth in 2.15–21. The thesis is then defended by a series of arguments or proofs: (*a*) An argument from indisputable evidence, 3.1–5; (*b*) An argument from scripture, 3.6–14; (*c*)

An argument from common human practice, 3.15–18; (*d*) A digression on the meaning of law for the Gentile church, 3.19–25; (*e*) An argument from the tradition of the church, 3.26–4.11; (*f*) An argument from friendship, 4.12–20; (*g*) Another argument from scripture, 4.21–31. The exhortation begins in 5:1.

Paul's thesis (2:15–21), summarized, is that Gentile Christians are not bound to keep the Torah of Israel. For Gentiles, the law can mean only one thing – condemnation. But in Jesus Christ, Gentiles have been given life. As John Gager notes, "Judaizing, not Judaism, is the issue" (Gager, 1983: 231). Paul never complains about the Torah, Jews or Jewish custom as practised by Jews. But Judaizing of Gentile Christians is inappropriate.

Our present passage cuts across the lines of the structure of the apologetic letter. It contributes to the explanation of the relationship of the law and the Gentiles in 3.23–25, and it shows how Gentiles are incorporated into the household of God in 3.26–28. Verse 29 serves as a summary. Paul seeks not to attack Judaism but to clarify the standing of the Gentiles before God and in their relationship to the law.

The passage presupposes that Gentiles were, indeed, "under the law" (3.23–25). The law was a "custodian" from which the Gentiles have only now, in Christ, been released. The question is, "What is the law to which the apostle makes reference?" It cannot be the law as Torah, since only Jews follow the Torah. Rather, Paul, here writing to Gentiles, uses the word law in its second sense in which it functions to condemn. Gaston makes the crucial point that the phrase "under the law" is found in no Jewish text to refer to the situation of Jews. Paul uses it exclusively to refer to the situation of Gentiles (Gaston, 1979: 62). They were under condemnation, and as such they were subject to the conditions of slavery described in 4.1–12. The Gentiles were released from condemnation only through Christ. "When Paul speaks of the law in this specific sense of how it relates to Gentiles, he says nothing whatsoever against the Torah of Israel or about the significance of the law for Jews or Jewish Christians" (Gaston, 1979: 52, cf. Gaston, 1984).

Verses 26–28 answer the question: "How do Gentiles come into the household of God?" They do so through baptism into Christ and not through the initiation rites prescribed in the Torah.

The closing verse helps to clarify the role of Abraham in Galatians (and in the whole of the Pauline corpus). Abraham is not an example whose faith is to be imitated by the Gentile Christians. Instead, Abraham is evidence from Scripture itself that Paul's gospel concerning the Gentiles is true. With the coming of the Gentiles to God through the church, the promises which God made to Abraham are shown to be true (Gager, 1983: 238–39; Gaston, 1980).

The sermon from this text will naturally call attention to the new context of interpretation (especially with regard to the law), and to the implications of the new interpretation for the Christian view of Judaism. For example, we can no longer castigate the Torah as a "custodian". The preacher will also want to remind the congregation of the good news which is inherent in the text. Once we Gentiles were under the law of condemnation. But now we have been freed and have become a part of the family of God through baptism. In this latter sense, the text has positive evangelistic power.

B. *Romans 7.14–25* occurs on the Seventh Sunday after Pentecost in Year A. In popular interpretation, the passage is taken as Paul's autobiographical statement of his own inner struggle brought about by the oppressive law of Judaism. This struggle was resolved only when Paul renounced Judaism with its enervating law and became a Christian. Thus preachers sometimes urge congregations to be thankful that they must no longer suffer under the law.

Three issues are basic to understanding this passage. First, is the chapter autobiographical? Secondly, how is the word "law" used in this passage? Thirdly, what is the relationship between sin and the law? How can the law excite sin?

Is Romans 7 autobiographical? Does it rehearse Paul's own inner struggle under the law? Several factors combine to call for a negative answer. Paul is not writing a verbatim account

of his psycho-history here but is using the pronoun "I" to speak
of the plight of the Gentiles under the law of condemnation.

In other passages where Paul speaks of his life as a Jew, prior
to his calling as apostle to the Gentiles, Paul makes no reference
to a "divided self" which was at war with its own members. In
an earlier chapter, we called attention to Paul's pattern of
speaking appreciatively of his own background in Judaism and
of the positive role of the law in that life. Paul even says that he
was blameless as to righteousness under the law (Philippians
3.6; cf. Galatians 1.13ff.). If Romans 7 is read autobiograph-
ically, Paul would be contradicting himself.

In Greek, the first person singular pronoun can represent a
larger group than simply the speaker. When so used, the
pronoun expressed an opinion which is taken to be valid
generally. A major New Testament Greek grammar sees the
use of the "I" in Romans 7 in this generalizing sense (Blass-
Debrunner: p. 147, par. 281). A comparable contemporary use
is the parent who says to the child, "I wouldn't do that!"

An important clue to the use of the pronoun "I" is Paul's
understanding of his apostolic vocation. A crucial passage
which bears directly on the interpretation of Romans 7 is I
Corinthians 9.20–22. Here, at the heart of Paul's vocation, is
the principle of identification with those to whom he goes.

The Letter to the Romans is addressed primarily to Gentiles.
As the apostle to the Gentiles, so great is Paul's identification
with the Gentile world that, while he never stops thinking of
himself as a Jew (e.g. Romans 11.1), he can use the first person
singular pronoun in its generalizing use and as a means of
identifying the situation of the Gentiles.

Scholars have long puzzled over the use of the word "law"
in Romans 7. Paul says some things about the law which are
quite affirmative (7.12, 14). Yet Paul also says some things
about the law that are quite negative (7.5). What is Paul's
attitude here?

The difficulty can be resolved when we remember that Paul
uses the word "law" in two different senses – one to refer to
the Torah, the gracious gift of God given to the covenantal
community Israel. The other use refers to the condition of the

Gentiles before God – accountable to God for fulfilling God's will yet not being a part of the covenantal community. In the latter case, the law can only function to condemn. Both uses appear in Romans 7 (see Gaston, 1979: 64–5).

On the one hand, Paul recognizes that the Torah is indeed holy and just and good (7.12, 13). The Torah is spiritual (7.14) and brings delight to the apostle (7.22).

On the other hand, Gentiles live in defiance of God's revealed will. Their story is given poignant expression in vv. 15, 18–20, 21, 23. Sin, which for Paul has autonomous power, actually takes advantage of the occasion of condemnation to increase its corruption of life-power. Hence Paul can say of the Gentiles, "Now if I do what I do not want, it is no longer I that do it but sin which dwells within me" (7.20). Even those occasions in which the Gentiles wish to do right are distorted by the presence of the "evil impulse" (7.21). No wonder chapter 7 rises to the bone-chilling cry, "Wretched man that I am! Who will deliver me from this body of death?" (7.24).

But death is not the final word, even for Gentiles. As 7.24ff. makes clear, Gentiles who come to God through Christ are no longer under condemnation (8.1) but are free from sin and death. Through Christ, God has made possible a new existence for Gentiles, one which is shaped by the working of the Spirit (8.4) and which may be characterized as life and peace (8.6).

In the sermon, the preacher will certainly want to clarify the two notions of law operative in this chapter and to portray the positive value of Torah as well as the negative function of condemnation. The text itself provides highly experiential characterization of Gentile life through statements like 7.15. How do we Gentiles daily experience the conflict which Paul portrays in these verses? The sermon should not close without a reminder that in Christ, God has delivered Gentiles from the body of death and has made possible a new existence through the Spirit, an existence of life and peace.

C. *Romans 11.13–16, 29–32* (Year A, the thirteenth Sunday after Pentecost) is one of only four readings from Romans 9–11 in the Common Lectionary. Therefore the preacher who chooses to stay within the bounds of the lectionary will need to take maximum use of this opportunity.

When working from these chapters, contemporary preachers often take the position that Jews will be saved *if* they become Christians. In some circles, the coming of the Jews to Christ is taken to be a sign of the "last days", the time of eschatological fulfilment. Other preachers, especially those with an ecumentical mind-set, believe that this is the proper interpretation of the passage, but are deeply offended by the idea of asking Jews to become Christian, so they avoid these chapters. Still other preachers find Paul's dense prose and torturous logic almost incomprehensible, and so they do not preach on Romans 9–11. Romans 9–11 offers the church a constructive theological resource for thinking about the relationship of Judaism and Christianity.

We begin with a survey on chapters 9–11 in the movement of Romans and with a statement of the overarching theme of these chapters. Against this background, the individual pieces within Romans 9–11, including 11.13–16, 29–32, can be read in a satisfying way.

Many scholars today agree with Krister Stendahl's understanding of Paul's magisterial letter. "What is the Epistle to the Romans about? It is about God's plan for the world and about how God's mission to the Gentiles fits into that plan" (Stendahl, 1976: 27). Chapters 1–8 function as a kind of "preface" to chapters 9–11 in order to show that in the mercy of God Jews and Gentiles can now come to God. The "preface" focuses principally on the way in which Gentiles may now be considered members of the household of God; they are justified by grace.

Romans 9–11 is not a footnote in the epistle but is its climax. Paul's overall point in these three chapters may be summarized thus. God has accepted both Jews and Gentiles. To be sure, the election of the Jews came first. But now, through Christ, God has brought Gentiles into fellowship with God's own self. Gentiles cannot boast that they are superior to Israel but can only stand in awe of the kindness of God.

Our passage confirms this overall theme and also introduces one of the complicating sub-themes of the argument, the rejection of Israel. Note that 11.13 identifies the passage as unmistakably directed to Gentiles and stresses Paul's apostleship to the Gentiles. Paul is thus seeking to help Gentile Christians to understand their relationship to Israel in the purposes of God.

What do the Jews reject in vv. 14–15? Since there is no suggestion in Romans (or elsewhere in Paul) that Jews must become Christian in order to enjoy fellowship with God, the best answer is that they resist acknowledging that the Gentiles are now children of God. Paul's remarkable claim is that this resistance actually worked for the advancement of the gospel!

The lectionary divides the reading in an unnatural place. The thought which is introduced in 11.13 continues in the analogy of the olive tree (Israel) into which the wild branches (Gentile Christians) have been grafted. The apostle is clearly *chiding the Gentiles* for having a superior (and mistaken) attitude toward such Jews. For "if you (Gentiles) have been cut off from what is by nature a wild olive tree, and grafted, contrary to nature, into a cultivated olive tree, how much more will these natural branches be grafted back into their own olive tree" (11.24). While Paul is sorry that some Jews have not recognized the kindness of God towards the Gentiles, the apostle is more concerned to see that Gentile Christians take no pleasure in that fact. God's electing grace will have the last word.

In 11.25, Paul confesses that the "hardening" of Israel towards the Gentile mission is a mystery. Here Paul uses the word "mystery" in its somewhat technical apocalyptic way to refer to the knowledge of events leading towards the eschaton (as in 1 Corinthians 2.7; 4.1; 13.2; 15.51). Thus, here, the coming of "the full number of Gentiles" to God is a sign of the eschatological age! A part of this age is also the salvation of all Israel (11.26). Indeed, according to 11.28–29, the salvation of Israel is secure because it rests on the love of a God whose gifts and call are irrevocable. God will have mercy on all (11.32).

We have now arrived at a position 180° from the popular conception of this section with which we began. Romans 9–11 does not call for Jews to become Christian. Paul might like Jews to recognize that through the grace of God in Jesus Christ,

Christians belong legitimately in the service of God. However, Paul is clear that Israel will be saved by virtue of the irrevocable call of God which is guaranteed by God's own faithfulness.

Further, contrary to the popular image, Paul does not teach that the coming of Jews to Christ is an eschatological sign. Quite the reverse. If we are to speak of an eschatological sign at all, we must speak of the conversion of Gentiles to God!

The sermon is certainly an occasion on which to correct the popular misapprehension of the text. It is also a time in which to make use of the image of the olive tree and its natural and grafted branches as a way of explaining the relationship of Judaism and Christianity and of highlighting the inappropriateness of missions to convert Jewish people to Christianity. Just as Christians need not become Jews in order to participate in the blessing of God, so Jews need not become Christians in order to continue in the blessing of God. The sermon can hardly by-pass the fundamental theological theme of God's mercy extended even to the disobedient.

Texts in need of correction

The following passages illustrate those which are inappropriate to the Christian witness in the way in which they represent Jews, Jewish practices, or God's love for Jews.

One time-honoured way of dealing with elements in the text which are anti-Jewish has been to see in these elements an analogy of the practices and attitudes of the contemporary church. For instance, the preacher might see the "legalistic Pharisee" and make an analogy with the legalism of the modern church. In the sermon, the congregation is asked to identify with the Pharisee. Even though this approach may soften the church's attitude of superiority towards Judaism, it is not a satisfactory solution to the problem because it leaves intact the historically inaccurate and theologically inappropriate picture of Judaism. In fact, the analogy simply reinforces the distorted picture of Jews and Judaism in the mind of the listener. A better approach to the appearance of anti-Judaism in the text is to

take the text as an occasion to point to the historical difficulty
and theological culpability of the text.

In homiletics classes, a criterion frequently employed in
criticism of the sermon is the norm of faithfulness to the biblical
text. "Was the preacher true to the text?" These texts challenge
that criterion. For to preach them, the preacher must speak
against Jews in such a way as to deny the heart of the gospel
message. A better criterion with which to begin the criticism of
the sermon is that of the gospel itself. "Was the preacher true
to the gospel?"

A. *Matthew 26.14–27.66* is a reading for Passion Sunday (the
Sixth Sunday in Lent) in Year A.

Until recently, in most recent liturgical calendars, Passion
Sunday was called Palm Sunday. Palm Sunday was regarded
as the beginning of the Holy Week services which day by day
followed Jesus' last week. Many years ago people went to church
daily during Holy Week and thus felt the gathering storm-
clouds which came to a head at the cross. Even after daily
worship died out, many churches continued to have large
congregations for Maundy Thursday communion and for Good
Friday services. On Palm Sunday, the congregation celebrated
the "triumphal entry" of Jesus into Jerusalem, and then on
Maundy Thursday and Good Friday the congregation walked
with Jesus into the darkening shadows. Only afterwards did
they hear the cry of victory, "He is risen!" By the time
Easter came the congregation had remembered the price of its
redemption.

In the last twenty years this situation has changed. Few
people in mainline churches come to church on Maundy
Thursday or Good Friday. This means that on Palm Sunday
they have an "up" and at Easter an "upper up", without
remembering the cross. In response, the church has created
Passion Sunday as a way of helping the congregation to recollect
the suffering love of God.

Yet this laudable move also has a significant liability with
respect to anti-Judaism. The Bible readings for the day are
among the most vitriolic and anti-Jewish documents from the
hand of the early church. Not only is the Jewish role in the

death of Jesus distorted, but the long Christian tradition of blaming Jews for the death of Jesus causes many of us to hear the Jewish elements as being more emphatic than they really are.

In this setting, the preacher will present the best of recent research into the circumstances surrounding the death of Jesus, the motivation for the Gospel accounts, and will help the congregations to understand that the death of Jesus can have saving significance for the church without casting impunity upon Jews past or present.

Contemporary scholarly investigation of the crucifixion of Jesus concludes that the Jewish community did not have the legal power to put people to death in the first century. The Romans, therefore, are legally responsible for the death of Jesus.

Although modern scholarship has found it difficult to establish exact detail, it appears that Jesus was put to death because the Romans perceived him as a threat to their political rule. It further appears that some Jews urged the Romans to come to this conclusion.

Whatever the exact circumstances surrounding the death of Jesus, Ellis Rivkin has refocused the question in a very helpful way. Instead of asking *who* killed Jesus, it is better to ask *what* killed Jesus. And what "emerges with great clarity, both from Josephus and from the Gospels, (is) that the culprit is not the Jews but the Roman imperial system" (Rivkin, 1984: 117). This system sucked even a few Jews into its service and crucified thousands of Jews, including Jesus, in the first century.

As we have noted earlier, the portrait of the Jews in the Gospels dates from the time of the fall of the temple and later, and reflects the conflict of the later churches with the Jewish communities of their own time. The mists of history and the polemical nature of the sources make it almost impossible to assess the historical accuracy of some of the details. For example, did Judas actually receive thirty pieces of silver from the chief priests in order to betray Jesus (Matthew 26.14)? The gospel writers use such details, whether historically factual or not, to inflame the mind of the reader against the Jews.

The Jews come as a violent mob with swords and clubs to

the garden to arrest Jesus (Matthew 26.47). This is in direct contrast to the Matthaean Jesus, who in 26.51–54 rejects the use of violence.

The trial before the Sanhedrin (26.57–68) is a key passage. For the purpose of discrediting the Jewish leaders, Matthew (and other Gospel writers) pictures the Sanhedrin as violating its own procedures. 1. The trial should be held in the daytime, whereas this one is held at night. 2. The trial should last for two consecutive days, whereas this one takes place in one night. 3. The trial should take place in the Hall of Hewn Stones, whereas this trial is held in the "living room" of the high priest. 4. The witnesses should be questioned privately, whereas here they are coached publicly. 5. The trial should begin with reasons for acquittal, whereas this trial begins with false testimony of guilt. 6. The witnesses should be cautioned concerning the accuracy of their testimony, whereas these witnesses are encouraged to give false testimony. The Christian interpreter, therefore, must face the fact that this is a false picture of Jewish trial practice.

The high priest tears his robe in a customary sign used when blasphemy is spoken. Technically speaking, Jesus has not committed blasphemy, yet the tearing of the robe is all it takes to incite the crowd to cry for the death of Jesus. The Jewish leaders and people fail to act according to their own rules.

The Jews prefer to have the notorious prisoner Barabbas on the streets than to have Jesus alive. Matthew 27.18–19 and 27.24 have the effect of whitewashing Pilate (who was known in the first century for the murder of thousands of Jews) while 27.20–23 and 27.25–26 place the blame for the death of Jesus squarely on the Jews. Pilate, a Gentile, has essentially declared Jesus to be innocent. The Jews, on the other hand, willingly accept responsibility for his death.

Matthew has left the Christian preacher in a terrible plight. The near-hero of this scene is Pontius Pilate, the murderer of thousands of Jews. The bright spot in the Matthaean passion narrative is the absence of the Pharisees among the Jewish characters depicted as manipulating the circumstances to take Jesus to the cross. This may be Matthew's way of keeping the door open for dialogue with the Pharisees of his own day.

Three questions are critical for the preacher. First, is Matthew's account of the trial of Jesus historically trustworthy? We have seen that this is not likely. In fact, like the other Gospel writers Matthew is motivated by theological polemic. Secondly, is Matthew's picture appropriate to the Gospel? Again, the response must be in the negative. Falsehood is never a part of the Christian witness. Thirdly, is it necessary to put the Jewish community in a bad light in order to speak of the saving power of the cross for the church? Again, the answer is "No". The claim that the death of Jesus is redeeming is not dependent upon anti-Judaism. When the death of Jesus is seen as the reason to castigate (and even to kill) Jews, the point of Jesus' death has been completely subverted. Passion Sunday is a good day on which to clear the air of misconceptions about the role of the Jews in the death of Jesus and the church's destructive attitude toward Jews.

B. *Luke 17.11–19* is read in year C on the Twenty-First Sunday after Pentecost or on Thanksgiving Sunday. The text is usually taken to contrast the gratitude of the one leper who returned to give thanks to Jesus with the ingratitude of the nine who did not return. However, when read in the light of its portrayal of Jews, the text is immediately recognized as a subtle statement of anti-Judaism. The Jews turn out to be not only ungrateful but unsaved. The liturgical calendar thus makes this passage especially insidious.

It appears that an earlier version of this story was a simple healing miracle, approximately parallel in form and content to Luke 5.12–16 (parallels in Mark 1.40–45 and Matthew 8.1–4). Someone, perhaps Luke, added the motifs of the return of the Samaritan and the ingratitude of the other nine.

As the text opens, Jesus is passing between Samaria and Galilee (v. 11). Lucan geographical detail nearly always has a theological purpose, and this detail alerts the reader to the Lucan concern to show that Samaritans (who join other Lucan characters in representing the religiously impure) are welcomed into the family of God through Jesus (cf. 10.25–37; Acts 1.1–11; 8.1–25). The masterful narrator of Luke-Acts frequently uses Samaritans as negative foils to the Jews. Where the Jews disregard the gospel and are even hostile to it, Samaritans usually welcome it.

The ten lepers live according to the prescription of Leviticus 13.45–56. They cry to Jesus, ". . . have mercy on us". Scholars are undecided as to whether this is a plea for healing or for alms. If it is the latter, the response of Jesus grants much more than their request. Their failure to return to give thanks casts an even darker light on the nine who did not come back.

Jesus tells the ten who are healed to go and show themselves to the priests, as Leviticus 13.49 says. On the way to the priests, they are healed. Since they are already going to the priests, they will easily be able to fulfil the requirements of Leviticus 14.1–32 about those who have been healed of leprosy. The central part of these rites includes the offering of sacrifice (Leviticus 14.10–20), which at least implicitly includes the giving of thanks to God!

The anti-Jewish twist begins when one of the ten returns to Jesus. Luke's masterful literary style brings the reader's full attention to focus on the sober words, "Now he was a Samaritan". In order to help the reader not to miss the anti-Jewish point, the author adds vv. 17–18.

The phrase "has made you well!" in the closing saying could also be translated "has saved you" (cf. 5.20; 7.50; 8.48; 18.42). The contrast, then, is probably between the Jews who received healing but not salvation and the Samaritan who received both (Betz, 1971: 325ff., cf. Fitzmyer, 1985: 1148–56).

The text provides the preacher with an excellent example which can show the congregation how anti-Judaism made its way into traditions which are not necessarily anti-Jewish. It is also an example of why anti-Judaism is not central to the meaning of many texts whose present content is anti-Jewish. The lepers who are healed (all ten of them) are already on their way to give thanks to God when one of them returns. The one who returns quite appropriately gives thanks to Jesus, but it is erroneous on Luke's part to suggest that the others would not otherwise give thanks to God. We can be glad for the Samaritan's healing and salvation, but these are not dependent on the rejection of the nine. In any case, in the season of thanksgiving, the preacher will best help the congregation not by berating them for ingratitude (especially at the expense of reinforcing anti-Judaism) but by helping the community remember its own healings and other reasons for offering thanks to God.

C. *Hebrews 5.5–10* is found in Year C on the Fourth Sunday of Advent. The text illustrates one of the difficulties of several of the Advent texts. On the one hand, they set forth the importance of the coming of Jesus. But on the other hand, they do so by downgrading Judaism. The implication is often that Christians rejoice because they no longer have to be Jews in order to enjoy fellowship with God.

Our reading is part of Hebrews 8–10 which, as we noticed on pp. 52ff., is built on the contrast between two covenants. One covenant is old, outmoded, pale, temporary and with the Jews. That covenant, with its constantly repeated rituals, is at best a shadow, a copy, of the real thing. But now that Jesus has come, the old covenant has been replaced by a new agreement which is described in terms almost the opposite of the terms of the old. It is new, permanent, made by a once-for-all sacrifice by an everlasting high priest.

Hebrews 10.5–10 makes its contribution to this argument by declaring that the sacrificial system of Judaism and the religion it represents are abolished. As the proof for this conclusion, the author cites two texts from the Septuagint which (the author believes) show that God has no desire or pleasure in sacrifice. In 10.5–7, the writer cites Psalm 40.6–8 and in 10.8 a proof text is given which is similar to several in the literature of Israel (e.g. I Samuel 15.23; Psalm 50.8; Isaiah 1.10–17; Jeremiah 7.21–26; Hosea 6.6). Hebrews 10.9 implies that only Jesus has truly fulfilled the purposes of God and hence according to 10.10 only through him is sanctification (i.e. access to God) possible.

In the season of Advent, the preacher is dealing with the question "What does the coming of Jesus mean?" Does Jesus' coming necessarily mean supersessionism, as this text claims? The preacher can use this text, and others like it, as a point of entry into the idea of supersessionism. Christians need not invalidate Judaism in order to validate our own religious convictions and practice. The good news of Advent, in the language of this text, is that our sanctification is dependent upon the grace of God revealed in Jesus.

D. *John 10.1–18* provides the readings for two Sundays in the Christian calendar. John 10.1–10 is the gospel reading for the Fourth Sunday of Easter in Year A while John 10.11–18 is the reading for the Fourth Sunday in Year B. These passages are so familiar, and so well loved, that one can easily overlook their biting anti-Judaism.

Chapter 10 presupposes the contrast between the true and false shepherds of Israel which was employed by many earlier writers in Israel (e.g. Ezekiel 34; Jeremiah 23.1–8; Zechariah 11.4–17; 13.7–9). The false shepherds lead the flock of God astray; at their worst, they eat the flock instead of feeding it. The true shepherds lead the flock in the ways of God, even when that way is difficult.

John 10.1–5 is an allegory using the images of the sheepfold and the sheepgate. The point of the allegory is very simple: one can get to the sheep the right way or the wrong way. The right way is to go through the door whereas the wrong way, taken by thieves and robbers, is to climb in through another way.

Verses 7–10 explain that Jesus is the sheepgate mentioned in the allegory. Entry to the sheepfold is through him, i.e., by becoming a Christian. According to v. 8, *all* others are thieves and robbers. The Pharisees of 9.41 are such false shepherds and thieves (10.22–39). When one enters the sheepfold through Jesus, one will be saved. But those who attempt to enter the sheepfold of God through other entries will be destroyed (10.9). The lovely line about abundant life (10.10) is thus a direct attack upon Judaism which, according to John, leads to death (cf. 6.49ff.; 8.24; 8.44).

John 10.11–18 claims that Jesus is now the *good* shepherd. He alone is the true way to God. Two reasons are given for seeing Jesus as the good shepherd. First, he lays down his life for the sheep, in contrast to the fearful hirelings who leave the sheep to the wolves (vv. 11–13). Secondly, the good shepherd knows the sheep intimately, even those Christians who are not in the Johannine church (vv. 14–18).

This passage presents the preacher with a complex challenge. The image of the good shepherd, inspiration of countless stained glass windows, is loved by many Christians. Yet one cannot deal with the text honestly without acknowledging that it denies God's friendship to the Jews and therefore is inappropriate to the basic premise of the gospel. On the other hand, the passages make several affirmations that are true to the experience of the church and should not be linked to anti-Judaism. For one thing, the world is still filled with false shepherds. Sheep need to know who they are. Further, for the church, Jesus is truly the gateway to God. The church does experience the shepherding care of God through Jesus. But the church can acknowledge that Jesus manifests these wonderful things without taking them away from Judaism. The line of logic which begins with the claim that God loves the *world* (John 3.16) calls for this very destination. Anything less involves John in an open self-contradiction.

In the Easter season the church is meditating on the purpose and power of God to bring life out of death. The church testifies to the continuing presence of the resurrected Jesus when it puts away anti-Judaism and affirms the life-giving power of God for all.

— 6 —

Sermons

Introduction

The following three sermons are examples of Christian preaching which attempt to address anti-Judaism in a direct way in the light of the gospel. "The Christian Minister as Teacher" illustrates one way of helping a congregation to recover a positive sense of the Jewishness of the formative Christian traditions. "There is One God, the Father" offers a model of addressing the relationship between the Jewish and Christian communities at the level of theological affirmation. "A Lesson in Humility" is an example of preaching against the text.

There is one God, the Father

Preached at the Indianapolis Hebrew Congregation 9 March 1985, on the occasion of Yom ha Shoah. *"Yom" is the Hebrew word for "day", and "Shoah" refers to a whirlwind of destruction, hence the day on which Jews remember those who died as martyrs in Hitler's "Final Solution of the Jewish Question".*

Your *Yom ha Shoah* service this year is designed to move from despair to hope, from *Kaddish* to *Kiddush*. This sermon is intended to move in the same direction. There is no point in my attempting to speak to you about the Holocaust. We are all familiar enough with Christian complicity in it and with the way Christian anti-Judaism laid the groundwork for it. We shall focus instead on hope, on the way in which Christian preaching and teaching are being reconstructed after the Holocaust. Let us do that by attending to a passage from one of Paul's letters, a slice of life from the history of the early church. Here is the text:

> Now concerning food offered to idols: we know that "all of us possess knowledge". "Knowledge" puffs up, but love builds up. If any one imagines that one knows something, one does not yet know as one ought to know. But if one loves God, one is known by God.
>
> Hence, as to the eating of food offered by idols, we know that "an idol has no real existence", and that "there is no God but one". For although there may be so-called gods in heaven or on earth – as indeed there are many "gods" and many "lords" – yet for us there is one God, the Father, from whom are all things and for whom we exist, and one Lord, Jesus Christ, through whom are all things and through whom we exist.
>
> However, not all possess this knowledge. But some, through being hitherto accustomed to idols, eat food as really offered to an idol; and their conscience, being weak, is defiled. Food will not commend us to God. We are no worse off if we do not eat, and no better off if we do. Only take care lest this liberty of yours somehow become a stumbling block to the weak. For if any one sees the one having knowledge sitting at table in an idol's temple, might one not be encouraged, if one's conscience is weak, to eat food offered to idols? (I Corinthians 8.1–9; RSV, modified slightly in the light of the Greek.)

This passage from Paul's First Letter to the Corinthians, written sometime during the sixth decade of the first century of the Common Era, shows us a cross-section of the life of the early church. Paul is dealing with the problem whether members of the church (they did not yet call themselves "Christians", nor did Paul ever so speak of them) might eat food that had been offered to idols. This problem was to plague the church for centuries.

Through the third and into the early fourth centuries, per-secutions of Christians by the Roman Empire grew in intensity. When we seek the reasons for these persecutions they seem to lie, fundamentally, in the distinctive life-style of Christians. The theologian Tertullian said in his *Apology*: "We have the reputation of living aloof from crowds."

Fundamental to the Christian life-style and the cause of endless hostility was the Christian rejection of the gods of the ancient world. The Greeks and Romans had deities for every aspect of living – for sowing and reaping, for rain and wind, for volcanoes and rivers, for birth and death, for entering and leaving a house. But to Christians (as to Jews) these gods were nothing, and their denial of them marked the followers of Jesus as "enemies of the human race", as their pagan critics called them. Christians shared this distinction, and the reasons for it, with Jews.

One simply could not reject the gods without arousing scorn as a social misfit. For the Roman, every meal began with a liquid offering and a prayer to the gods. Christians could not participate in that. Most dinner parties and feasts were held in the precincts of a temple, after sacrifice had been made, and the invitation was usually to dine "at the table" of some god. Christians could not accept. Inevitably they seemed stand-offish, exclusive. They got into trouble in Roman society because they were pretty good Jews – better than they knew, usually. Occupations were closed to Christians: they could not be school teachers, because they could not tell the stories of the gods that were part of the civil religion of the time. They could not work in hospitals (such as they were), because such work was dedicated to Asclepius, the god of healing.

Everywhere Christians turned in pagan society, they were on display, standing out like so many sore thumbs. Like Jews, they were bound to divorce themselves from the social and economic life of the times. Their faithfulness to one God, interpreted by outsiders as aloofness or exclusivism, lay at the root of their eventual persecution by Rome and was why they would not engage in the emperor-worship, which was only the more proximate cause of their difficulties.

Christians, then, for several hundred years were better Jews than they knew and than their heirs have given them credit for being. And they paid a considerable price for it, one that included a lot of Christian lives. Yet already in Paul's time we find that some "super-smart" Gentile followers of Jesus *thought* that they had the answer to this problem and that it was an easy answer.

Paul says of them in our passage that they "possess knowledge". These smart people did indeed possess knowledge; they made a good argument. Paul accepted their premise, but rejected their conclusion. In their debate with Paul on eating meat offered to idols they contended that idolatry was a matter of indifference. After all, they said, you and we both know that the idols do not really exist; "there is no God but one". Paul quite agrees with them on this point, but takes a different tack. He argues against them that people of strong conscience should be concerned for their weaker brothers and sisters, who might be led to think that idolatry is a matter of indifference. Paul here instructs his congregation about its behaviour, providing a rabbinic ruling about what they should do.

In the process, Paul makes an important theological remark. I'll cite it again, and as I do I encourage you to pay attention to the prepositions in it. Having referred to the "so-called" gods and lords of pagan society, Paul says: "Yet for us there is one God, the Father, *from* whom are all things and *for* whom we exist, and one Lord, Jesus Christ, *through* whom are all things and *through* whom we exist."

On both points Paul reacted as a good first-century Jew, one who may have studied under Gamaliel (Acts 22.3). On eating meat offered to idols, he decides *not* to have Christians assimilate to pagan customs and to the predominant *mores* of the society. He knows that the idols represent *nothing*, that the "so-called" gods do not exist. Yet that does not make honouring them a matter of indifference. Paul is stubbornly Jewish on this point. What I want to show now is that he was also stubbornly monotheistic in his other insistence, that there is only one God, *from* whom are all things, and one Lord, Jesus Christ, *through* whom are all things.

The question we must ask ourselves is what Paul means by this statement. First, we should note that Paul does *not* say that Jesus is the Messiah. The term "Messiah" (in Greek *Christos*) did not have in Greek the meaning that it did in Hebrew and Aramaic. It meant "the oily head". To say of someone that he is the oily head is no big deal. So by the time of Paul (who, I remind you, is our *first* Christian writer), the term "Messiah" had been played down as a title for Jesus because with it the church could not express his significance. Messiah, instead, became a name of Jesus. Hence, Paul says that Jesus Christ (Jesus Messiah) is Lord – because only in *this* way can he say what he wants to say about the significance of Jesus.

What did he want to say? To begin with, we must note that Paul is not simply making a claim; he is making a counter-claim. He has referred to "the so-called gods in heaven or on earth" and has also said that "indeed there are many gods and many lords". These so-called gods actually exist. There is no contradiction here. The formal meaning of the term "god" or "lord" is what constitutes any person's ultimate concern – what you finally, ultimately trust, what in the last ditch is the ultimate ground of your self-understanding as a person. In other words, what is it that you are willing to trust as finally fulfilling your life as a human being and under the ultimate demand of which you are willing to place yourself? In this sense, whatever you choose to invest with ultimacy in relation to your own existence is *your* "god" or "lord".

This is what Luther meant in his *Large Catechism*, when he said that "the trust and faith of the heart alone make both God and an idol. . . . For these two belong together, faith and God. That to which your heart clings and entrusts itself is, I say, really your God." This does not mean that we have the power to decide whether God exists. God *is*. Yet, in the existential sense, God only is *for you* and *for me* when in our own freedom we choose to exist *for God* by existing as authentic human beings.

We have the opportunity to understand ourselves authenti-cally, which means finally in terms of, and only in terms of, God's love for each and all, oneself included, and therefore also in terms of God's command for justice to each and all of those whom God loves. But we also have the freedom to *mis*-understand ourselves. Not everything that we in fact choose to trust with the final meaning of our lives is really trustworthy. It is possible for us to live in terms of realities that are not the reality from and through which all things exist and for and through which we are to live our lives. There are indeed many gods and many lords.

Everywhere we turn there are people who understand the ultimate meaning of their lives as based in some less than ultimate reality. We do not necessarily have to look outside churches and synagogues to find these people; sometimes we can find them inside, perhaps across the aisle. The best place to look, however, is in the mirror. Where do we find the ultimate meaning of our lives, what we are willing to trust, finally? Do we find our final ground of security in our national military posture? Is what really counts the macho superiority of those of us who are male? Or are our heart's devotions focussed on our investment portfolio? Have we, in the words of Rabbi Yeshua ha Notzri, laid up treasures for ourselves on earth, where moth and rust consume and thieves break in and steal? Do we worship the bitch goddess success? Whenever we find the ultimate meaning of our lives in anything other than the one true God alone, the God of Israel, we in effect worship at the shrine of some so-called god or lord that has no real existence as the divinity we take it to be through our idolatrous devotion. If we put our ultimate trust in nuclear missiles, we should face the fact that all idols make an ultimate demand upon us – in this case a nuclear demand. A difference between idols and the one true God is that the fulfilment offered by idols is destructive, whereas that offered by God is creative.

It is as a counter-claim to idolatrous faith in many gods and many lords that Paul offers his concise statement of the faith of the church. And while idolatry is as real a problem for Jews as for Gentiles, to understand Paul we have to remember that he never wrote to Jews advising them on these matters, but only to Gentiles. Hence, for example, Paul never urges Gentiles to *return* to God, because they did not know God. Instead, he urges them to turn to God for the *first* time. Paul is talking to Gentiles in the church. Like Jews, Gentiles receive the gracious gift of life itself *from* God. God is the creative ground of life, the gracious presence in its midst, and the final goal redemptive of it all, the Alpha and the Omega. But it is *through* Jesus Christ, the preaching of the gospel of Jesus Christ in and by the early church, that Gentiles came to know of God, through Jesus Christ that they – we – came to understand ourselves in terms of God as the ultimate ground of our lives. Jews had come to this understanding earlier, through the action of God in the life of Israel and through the Torah.

When Paul says that there is one God from whom are all things and one Lord Jesus Christ through whom are all things, he is not discussing issues in the trinitarian debates that are two and three centuries later than him in time. He is not affirming that two divine beings are the object of Christian faith, nor is he subordinating Jesus Christ to God the Father. Rather, for Paul the reality declared by the words "God our Father" is one and the same with that shown forth as "our Lord Jesus Christ". What it means to have God as our Father existentially is the same as having Jesus Christ as our Lord. What it means to have Jesus Christ as our Lord existentially is the same as having God as our Father. The significance of Jesus Christ is that through him we Christians understand ourselves in relationship to God.

Jews and Christians are in the same boat. The problem we both face is idolatry – understanding ourselves ultimately in terms of what is only finite and relative. According to a story we remember, while Moses was receiving the Torah the people were making a golden calf, understanding themselves in terms of gold and fertility – hardly authentic. We still have a problem today not to identify what we ultimately trust with money and sex. Yet down the long millennia while Jews were being schooled in the Torah, my ancestors were worshipping Wotan, doing strange things with stone monoliths, painting their faces blue, and baying at the moon. Their fertility deities were Maeve and Fergus – an interesting couple.

In the language of one of Paul's first-century students, during all this time we Gentiles were "alienated from the commonwealth of Israel, and strangers to the covenants of promise, having no hope and without God [*atheoi*] in the world. But now in Christ Jesus you [Gentiles] who once were far off have been brought near in the blood of Christ. For he is our peace who has made us both one, and has broken down the dividing wall of hostility . . ." (Ephesians 2.12–15).

Through Jesus Christ we Gentiles come to understand ourselves in relation to God the Father, the covenant God of Israel who was disclosed in Israel's history, through the law and the prophets, as the God of a unique promise and command. The *promise* is the free and unconditioned offer of God's love as the only proper ground for our self-understanding. The *command* is that by so understanding ourselves we shall be freed to fulfil the law, which is all summed up in the one sentence. "You shall love your neighbour as yourself." Jesus Christ re-presents the same promise and command previously re-presented in the Exodus and on Mount Sinai. What it means to have Jesus Christ as Lord is to have the covenant God of Israel as the gracious and commanding ground and end of our being. The word addressed to each of our communities in its central revelatory event – Mt Sinai or Mt Calvary – is *precisely* the same word.

The news from Sinai and from Calvary is good. The word is and the point is that because God is one, God is not the God of Jews only, but of Gentiles also. This God who loves us both commands us to love and do justice to one another.

On this commemoration of *Yom ha Shoah*, it is certainly more than time for us, particularly us Christians, to heed this command.

The Christian minister as teacher

This sermon was preached on 6 May, 1984 at the Meadlawn Christian Church, Indianapolis, on the occasion of the ordination of Ms Rene Jensen to the Christian ministry.

And one of the scribes came up and heard them disputing

with one another, and seeing that he answered them well, asked him, "Which commandment is the first of all?" Jesus answered, "The first is, 'Hear, O Israel: The Lord our God, the Lord is one; and you shall love the Lord your God with all your heart, and with all your soul, and with all your mind, and with all your strength.'

The second is this, 'You shall love your neighbour as yourself.' There is no other commandment greater than these." And the scribe said to him, "You are right, Teacher; you have truly said that he is one, and there is no other but he: and to love him with all the heart and all the understanding, and with all the strength, and to love one's neighbour as oneself, is much more than all whole burnt offerings and sacrifices." And when Jesus saw that he answered wisely, he said to him, "You are not far from the Kingdom of God." And after that no one dared to ask him any question (Mark 12.28–34).

A careful study of this passage from the earliest Gospel shows us how thoroughly Jewish was this teacher from Nazareth. The conversation reported between him and "one of the scribes" is so Jewish in content and tone that we Gentiles have a hard time listening for the quality and pitch of what is said. The scribe addresses Jesus as *didaskale*, teacher/master, "rabbi" translated into Greek. Jesus' answer compels the scribe, responding out of the depths of his own historical identity, to call Jesus a truth-teller. It was important to the scribe to ascertain that Jesus was telling the truth, and it was important to Jesus to tell it. The scribe acknowledges Jesus as a true teacher of Israel, and Jesus proclaims that the scribe is not far from the *Basileia*, the reign, of God.

This, however, only scratches the surface of the thorough-going Jewishness of this text. Jesus introduces the Great Commandment with the famous words, "Hear, O Israel, the Lord our God is one Lord." This is the proclamation "*Shema, Yisrael, adonai elohenu, adonai ehad*'", the closest thing Judaism had or has to a creed and which is heard today in every service in every synagogue of the people Israel. The deep Jewish resonance of this remark was embarrassing to the church of the later first century. Both Matthew and Luke dropped it from their accounts of the same story.

This evidence that the *Shema* was discomfiting to the later church is testimony to its authenticity as a saying of Jesus; Mark preserves this confession of Jesus in spite of those concerns which later led Matthew and Luke to omit all mention of it. Mark shows us how Jewish this rabbi from Nazareth really was. This Jesus whose Hebrew/Aramaic name is a short sentence – *Joshua, Yeshua*, meaning "Yahweh is salvation" – opens his summary of the law with Israel's classic confession.

Again, the Jewishness of what Jesus said and did is evident in the fact that he says nothing new in these words. He merely quotes some verses of scripture and links them together. The first set is Deuteronomy 6.4–5; "Hear, O Israel: the Lord our God is one Lord: and you shall love the Lord your God with all your heart, and with all your soul, and with all your might." The second is Leviticus 19.18b: "You shall love your neighbour as yourself."

Jesus and the scribe address each other as Jews, out of the depths of the Jewish experience of God. Jesus introduces his answer to the scribe with the *Shema*. The content of the answer itself is thoroughly Jewish, consisting only of two quotations from what the Bible itself calls, simply, "the scriptures".

But surely, you will say, at least in his reduction of all the law to two commandments Jesus is atypical of Judaism. Not even in this respect, however, does he depart in the slightest from the Judaisms of his time.

We find the Jewish writer Philo of Alexandria, who lived from about 20 BCE to about 54 CE, an older contemporary of Jesus, saying much the same thing:

And there are, so to speak, two fundamental teachings to which the numberless individual teachings and statements are subordinated: in reference to God the commandment of honouring God and piety, in reference to humanity that of the love of humanity and justice (*Concerning Individual Commandments*, II, 63).

The Testament of Daniel declares, "Love the Lord in your
whole life and one another with a sincere heart" (5.3). It is the
rabbinic comment on the matter, however, which takes the
cake:

> Rabbi Simlai said, 613 commandments were given to Moses,
> 365 negative commandments, answering to the number of
> days of the year, and 248 positive commandments, answering
> to the number of a man's members. Then David came and
> reduced them to eleven (Psalm 15). Then came Isaiah, and
> reduced them to six (Isaiah 33.15). Then came Micah and
> reduced them to three (Micah 6.8). Then Isaiah came again,
> and reduced them to two, as it is said, "Keep ye judgment
> and do righteousness." Then came Amos, and reduced them
> to one, as it is said, "Seek ye me and live." Or one may say,
> then came Habakkuk (2.4), and reduced them to one, as it is
> said, "The righteous shall live by his faith" (*A Rabbinic
> Anthology*, ed. Montefiore and Loewe, p. 199).

Just prior to the time of Jesus, the great liberal teacher Hillel
had the following story told of him: "A heathen came to
Shammai, and said to him, 'Accept me as a proselyte on the
condition that you teach me the whole law while I stand on one
foot.' Then Shammai drove him away with the measuring rod
which he held in his hand. Then he went to Hillel, who received
him as a proselyte and said to him. 'What is hateful to you do
not to your fellow: that is the whole law; all the rest is its
explanation; go and learn.' "
In one last feature this story of Jesus is nothing but a Jewish
story: in the radical monotheism which Jesus repeats here:
"The Lord our God is one Lord." Martin Buber suggested that
the kind of love of God commands is monotheistic. As God is
one, so should we become one by loving God with all dimensions
of ourselves. Monotheism is an act at least as much as it is a
belief, and perhaps more.
Also, of course, there is no other God. Existentially we all
still have difficulty with this point, choosing at times to worship
the pocket-book or sex or nationalism, but it is true. There is

no other. It is no wonder that the scribe told Rabbi Yeshua,
"You have said the truth."

What has all this Jewish stuff to do with the Christian
ministry? We Christians have from Jesus Christ three functions
of ministry: the prophetic, the priestly and the royal. That is,
we see Jesus respectively as teacher, as reconciler and as servant,
exercising his royalty in washing the disciples' feet. So we in
our ministries must teach, must reconcile and must serve,
thereby re-presenting the gospel of Christ to the church and to
the world. But note that reconciling and serving are active
forms of teaching the Christian faith, setting forth what it means
to live the Christian life, while teaching in the ordinary sense is
the verbal edge of a pattern of activity.

So we learn from this story a model for teaching. Jesus taught
out of the depths of his heritage and not in violent reaction
against it. He participated in a creative transformation of that
heritage, as did others at his time. He taught both the love of
God for us and for all and the command of God for justice,
never just half a gospel, no mini-theology.

From Jesus we who would teach the Christian faith learn the
criteria of a good teacher. In Mark 12 the theme of Jesus as
teacher is strongly present. Earlier in that chapter Mark had
said: "And they sent to him some of the Pharisees and some of
the Herodians to entrap him in his talk. And they came and
said to him, 'Teacher, we know that you are true, and care for
no one: for you do not regard the position of men, but truly
teach the way of God. Is it lawful to pay taxes to Caesar, or
not' " (Mark 12.13–15)? This story is widely misunderstood by
Christians. It involves the criteria for the truthful teacher for
which the question of the taxes serves merely as an illustration.
We, who are devoutly interested in taxes, usually take them as
the main point of the story.

Jesus' colleagues think him worthy of being submitted to a
serious theological test and he is willing to take it. They and he
take one another seriously as teachers in Israel. This test is not
necessarily hostile, but it is probing and among colleagues
entirely proper. This text names three criteria for the good
teacher. "You care for no one" is better stated: "You do not

court anyone's favour." The good teacher, and only the good teacher is the real teacher, is marked by an ethos of independence based in large part on personal character.

The second criterion is hardly translated at all by the Revised Standard Version. It is: "You do not look people in the face." This is a strange remark. Someone of whom this is said today would be thought of as shifty-eyed, unscrupulous. But in the time of Jesus, to say that a teacher did not look people *eis prosopon*, in the face, meant something different. To look people in the face meant to look at them in order to find out what to say that will be pleasing. Such a teacher would teach only what people want to hear. Jesus was not such an inauthentic teacher.

The third criterion is: "You teach the way of God in truth." Jesus teaches *the way of God*, and not another way. What is the way of God? That we should love the Lord our God with all we have and our neighbours as ourselves. This is the way of life long ago declared in Deuteronomy: "I call heaven and earth to witness against you this day, that I have set before you life and death; therefore, choose life, that you and your descendants may live" (30.19).

So there you have it: a commission to be a Christian teacher, a model, and the criteria. Court no one's favour. Do not make your teaching dependent on what you see on people's faces. Teach the way of God truthfully. In the grace of God, this is what ministers are given and called to do.

A lesson in humility

Luke 18.9–14

The following sermon was prepared for a group of clergy. This accounts for the in-house talk that one would not find in a sermon given to the usual Sunday-morning congregation.

Have you noticed an interesting thing about Bible study? You can work on a text, get a good, strong handle on its meaning, write up your notes and put them in a manila folder and close the file drawer of your mind on it. Then, you come back to that text at a later time, and you can get out your notes, and – is that the same text? There are things in it that you didn't see at all before. And some of the things that you saw framed in neon lights are now almost invisible. I am old enough now to know that this happens not just once or twice, but again . . . and again . . . and again.

I used to think I had just the right set of notes on the parable of the Pharisee and the tax collector. This is a story, I thought, about the arrogant, self-righteous Pharisee and the penitent, humble tax collector. The Pharisee is the villain, and the tax collector is the hero, and my job is to emulate the hero.

Can you imagine the gall of this Pharisee, standing up in front of God and all the people in the temple and reading the roll of his own good works? "I am not an extortioner. I am not unjust. I am not an adulterer. I am not (and spoken with disgust in his voice) like this tax collector. And look at this. I fast twice a week and I tithe everything." It just drips of arrogance. Or so I thought.

Now I could understand why he felt so self-confident. After all, he was a Jew, and we all know that Jews believe that one can earn God's favour by good works. And the Pharisees were the Jews of the Jews. They had rules to cover everything from bestiality to what to do with mint and cumin. The ten commandments were chicken-feed to them. And this man was a Pharisee's Pharisee. He is confident that all his good works had earned him a place in God's favour, and so he stands there in the temple just dripping of arrogance and self-righteousness.

In contrast, look at the humility of the tax collector. He won't even come to the front of the temple area or lift up his eyes. He stands at the back of the temple and beats his breast – a traditional Jewish gesture for penitence. And listen to this simple, honest, heartfelt prayer. "God, be merciful to me, a sinner."

It was easy to preach a sermon from that perspective. All I needed to do was point out the fate of these two characters, and why they turned out that way, and then apply the conclusion to the congregation. The tax collector went down to his house justified but the Pharisee did not. And why? Because all who exalt themselves (like the Pharisee) will be humbled, and all who humble themselves (like the tax collector) will be exalted. Now, put the question to the congregation. How would *you* rather turn out – like the Pharisee or like the tax collector? Of course, you would rather turn out like the tax collector, so you need to humble yourselves. Down with self-righteousness. Up with penitent self-humiliation. And, of course, the congregation cast their eyes down and started beating their breasts and tried to feel humble.

But then knowledge befell me. This way of thinking about the parable contains errors. One of them is theological. An underlying idea of the parable is that we can cause our own justification by developing a proper attitude of humility. Humility and penitence thereby turn into works that earn justification. This, of course, is just the opposite of the basic affirmation of the Christian faith, namely, that God freely and graciously justifies all, especially those who are least deserving of it, Pharisee and publican alike.

Another problem is a strange inversion which takes place when the story is read this way. Those who see the tax collector as the hero and model almost always end up *exalting humility*. Yes, we modern-day people often wear our humility with the very same self-righteousness and arrogance that we attribute to the Pharisee in the story. And so we become like the very character we dislike.

Aha, I thought. These insights go along with the modern approach to the parables which sees the parables as exploding the world-view of the listeners. I have identified with the tax collector when I should have been identifying with the Pharisee because it is the Pharisee's world which is exploded by the parable. This led to another way of interpreting the story.

In contemporary terms, we mainline church members are like the Pharisee in the story. Someone calls the Pharisee the "religious insider" (Granskou: 104), the person who presumes to understand and to practise the purposes of God. He is the chair of the board of directors, the Sunday School teacher or choir member with twenty-three years of perfect attendance, the person who cleans up after every social event. And a

wonderful quality of the caricature is that it applies equally
well to persons on the left as well as on the right. You can be a
Pharisee for world peace as much as for your country.

The self-satisfied world-view of the Pharisee is smashed by
the treatment given in the story to the tax collector, the person
of deplorable moral behaviour who is a civic menace. Who is
the modern analogue to the tax collector? The alcoholic and
the drug dealer? The pimp and the whore? The child abuser?
The person who contracted Aids in a men's room in a bus
station? The defence contractor who makes big money by
manufacturing instruments of death? The stockholders in the
gold mines in South Africa?

According to this parable, these tax collectors come to church
and sit under the shadow of the balcony on the back row. The
preacher wonders why she can never make eye-contact with
them. But when the service is over, they go home with the peace
of God in their hearts, whereas the elders and deacons go home
to another night of anxious tossing and turning and Valium.
And why? Because the tax collectors of the world know their
need of God. When everything is stripped away – the trappings
of power, the money, the drugs, the booze, the sex – when
everything is stripped away, they know that the only thing they
have is God.

That certainly exploded the world-view of a few small-town
chamber-of-commerce-type elders.

And yet, this approach does not take full account of the best
of our knowledge of Pharisees and publicans in the first century.
The Pharisee, you see, was a pillar of the community, a
progressive, a lay reformer who sought to make religion vital in
the heart and in behaviour. When we read the writings produced
by the Pharisees, we find them rejoicing in the grace which has
been given to them and in the law which is God's wonderful
gift of instruction for the world.

And when we look at the qualities of the Pharisee's life which
are enumerated in the brief prayer in the parable, we see that
they are all good qualities. He does not rip people off through
extortion. He does not cheat on his spouse. He practises justice.
He fasts, which is a form of spiritual discipline and prayer, and

he tithes. These things are good for his own spiritual life and for the life of the community.

Now let me ask you this. How many of you are so moved by the need of the world and by your own spiritual hunger that you fast once a year, let alone twice a week? And how many of you tithe . . . your *gross* income?

The German scholar Joachim Jeremias has found several texts from first-century Pharisees which contain prayers much like this one. The dominant tone in all of them is thanksgiving for the wonderful presence and work of God. I cannot find any suggestion of arrogance or self-righteousness. Rather, they are honest, plain-spoken expressions of thanks to God for the gift of grace and the life which the law makes possible. Jeremias, who was no friend of Pharisees, even asks: "What fault can be found with his prayer?" (Jeremias: 143).

The publican, on the other hand, made his living by collecting taxes. As you know, the tax collectors were assigned a certain amount of money to bring to Caesar. In order to stay in the tax-collecting business they had to raise that amount. Anything more that the tax collectors could collect was profit, and so tax collectors habitually ripped off their clients in order to fatten their own pockets. And, of course, as a Jew in the employ of Rome, he was profiting by keeping in place the political power which was oppressing his own people. This man is immoral in his personal dealings and is a threat to the public welfare. The parable itself contains no hint that the publican ever mended his ways. How can he be a model for the Christian community just because he comes to church and beats his breast? You know what we call that? Cheap grace. Where is the life of justice which is practised by the Pharisee?

So what do we have here? We have a story which denigrates Jews and which exalts tax collectors who repent but give no other sign of new life. This runs contrary to the gospel of God, which promises God's love to each and all and commands that justice be done to each and all. Here we have a story that denies God's love to the Pharisee (who lives a life of justice) and which affirms God's love for the tax collector but expects no justice on his part. Does this story explode a world-view? You bet it does. It explodes the world of common sense.

What is the purpose of the story? And does it have any good news for us, today?

Since you are all familiar with the modern, critical interpretation of the Bible, I can get right to the point. Luke uses this story as a way of doing two things. First, it discredits the Pharisees (Jews). Luke does not see them as an authentic spiritual force in the first century. As the text says, they are people who "trust in themselves". The church of Luke's time was in a conflict with the synagogue, and this story is a way of saying, "Look at the Jews; they are like this Pharisee." Secondly, the story reminds Luke's church that even tax collectors receive God's grace and are welcome in God's church.

Luke was wrong and right. Like political cartoonists of today, Luke has created a caricature of the Pharisee for the purpose of getting the members of his church to believe that the Pharisees are empty shells, braggarts, and are no longer God's friends. This is dishonest. It is dishonest with respect to both the Pharisees and to God. And as long as we continue to act as if the story were a true representation of the Pharisees of the ancient world and of God's attitude towards Jews, we will continue to be dishonest. There is no need for us to stand far off and keep our eyes downcast and beat our breasts. But we do need to change the way in which we talk about the Pharisee in the story and the way we talk about Jews in the world of the first century.

But Luke got it right, too. God still welcomes tax collectors and sends them home justified. Of course, we should add that all who accept God's justification will want to live in just ways. The promise of God's love carries within it the command of God's justice. This is good news! And, yes, it is for the alcoholic and the drug dealer, the pimp and the whore, the child abuser and the homosexual. Yes, it is for the defence contractor and the stockholders in the gold mines. And yes, it is for the Pharisees.

And do you know what? The way I used to interpret this story was . . . immoral . . . and a threat to the public welfare.

But since God still welcomes tax collectors, then God welcomes me . . . *even* me. And if that isn't a lesson in humility, nothing is!

Eliminating Anti-Judaism from Worship

Introduction

Anti-Judaism often makes its way into the prayers, hymns, responsive readings and symbolic gestures of public worship. In liturgical material, anti-Judaism is often more subtle than in the Bible and in preaching, but its effect is no less damaging. In this chapter, we identify some common examples of anti-Judaism and suggest remedies.

A test which can be put to each part of the service is to ask, "Does this hymn, this prayer, this responsive reading represent Judaism in a truthful way? Does it affirm God's love for each and all and does it presuppose that God's justice should be done for each and all?"

The selection of the Bible readings

The Bible readings in worship are usually chosen by the preacher of the day either completely freely or from an established lectionary. Both methods of selection contain the possibility of anti-Judaism.

The method of *free selection* is especially vulnerable. Unless parish preachers are especially watchful and critical, they may begin to ride "hobby horses" in their selection of texts and themes, turning week after week to the same biblical writers or to texts which manifest similar themes. This is extremely limiting. Furthermore, because most preachers prefer texts from the last twenty-seven books of the Bible, these hobby horses can easily be anti-Jewish. Because of this same preference, preachers can overlook texts from the life of Israel. The congregation is thus denied access in public worship to the rich heritage of the formative literature of Judaism.

Those who select texts freely need to see that the congregation is exposed generously to the stories of Israel and to guard against a steady diet of anti-Jewish texts. When an anti-Jewish text is read, its theological difficulty can become the occasion for teaching.

The modern *lectionaries* are rightly praised for their several strengths. (For discussion of these strengths, see Bailey; Skudlarek: 11–63; Bower; 15–41.) But the lectionaries currently in use do little to enhance our appreciation of Judaism and they contribute to the problem of anti-Judaism.

James A. Sanders points to several ways in which the modern lectionaries frustrate Christian appreciation of Judaism.

1. The readings from the Hebrew Bible are "subordinated in Christian lectionaries to at best a supporting role" to the passages from the literature from the hand of the early church (Sanders, 1983: 258). In most lectionaries, the functional hermeneutic which governs the relationship between the readings from the Hebrew Bible and the readings from the gospels and letters is that of prophecy (anticipation, yearning) which is fulfilled and completed only in the story of Jesus. In some instances, Christianity becomes the type of which Judaism is the antitype. The reading from the life of Israel is not valued for its own sake or in its own integrity.

2. Not surprisingly, then, the lectionaries "perpetuate a Christocentric reading of the Bible as a whole" (Sanders, 1983: 259). The lectionary, with the Gospel reading as the primary reading for the day, leaves the impression that the whole Bible points to Christ. This is especially unfortunate when the gospel reading is shot-through with anti-Judaism, thus communicating the idea that the Christian religion itself is anti-Jewish. In mature Christian theology, Christ is not the goal but is the means whereby *God* is revealed and made accessible to the Christian community.

3. Consequently, lectionaries implicitly suggest that God's

real action did not begin until Jesus. The stories of God's activity in Israel are functionally regarded as a "preface" to God's work in Christ. Yet, as Sanders notes, "As a biblical scholar, I must emphasize that New Testament writers never intended to tell the whole truth. They presupposed that its readers knew their scripture, which was solely Old Testament, or much of what we call the Old Testament" (Sanders, 1983: 259).

At bottom, the issue is the degree to which we honour the integrity of the first thirty-nine books of the Bible and the activity of God which they represent.

Furthermore, in the modern lectionaries, the congregation is not given wide exposure to the texts which came to us from Israel. On a given Sunday, two of the three readings are taken from the literature from the early church and only one reading is taken from the Law, the Prophets or the Writings of Israel. (This is despite the fact that the Hebrew Bible is four times the length of the canonical apostolic writings.) In most lectionaries, the passages from the sacred scriptures of Judaism are cut and pasted into the lectionary apart from any sense of context and continuity. One week the reading might be from Leviticus, another week from Isaiah and another week from Job. Even the Common Lectionary, which attempts to address the problem of continuity by using representative, sequential readings from the historical narratives, the prophets and the wisdom litera-ture, cuts and slices the material, and omits many, many significant passages. Hebrews, one of the most anti-Jewish documents in the canon, is read almost in its entirety. Yet only ten small snippets from the stories of the ancestral families in Genesis are included, and these are not read in sequence. Consequently, the worshipping community never gets the sense of the unfolding drama of Abraham and Sarah, Isaac and Rebekah, Jacob, Leah and Rachel, Joseph.

The preacher can do several things to help ameliorate this situation. First, if the length of the service allows for only two scripture readings, the reading from the Hebrew Bible can always be included. Secondly, the pastor can frequently select the readings from the Hebrew Bible as the text for the sermon.

A minimum goal might be once a month. Thirdly, services can be organized around themes and images from the canonical writings of Israel.

Most of the modern lectionaries are based on the principle of *lectio selecta* (readings which are selected because of the way in which they illuminate the basic themes of the Christian Year – Advent, Christmas, Lent, etc.). But another principle on which lectionaries have been organized in the past is the *lectio continua*, the continuous reading of whole books of the Bible. The Common Lectionary attempts to combine these two principles, using the principle of *selecta* from Advent through Pentecost Day and a version of *continua* in the season of Pentecost. While the results are fairly satisfactory in the case of the gospels and epistles, they are quite unsatisfactory in the case of the literature of Israel. The church could commit itself to reading continuously through whole books of the canonical Jewish literature.

Referring to the parts of the Bible

Christian custom is to refer to the first thirty-nine books of the Bible as the Old Testament and the last twenty-seven books as the New Testament. Those churches which regard the apocryphal books as canonical sometimes refer to them as the Apocrypha and sometimes include them as a part of the Old Testament. Yet, the nomenclature of "old" and "new" contributes to anti-Judaism.

In our culture, "old" is often a negative word denoting that which is wearing out, outmoded, no longer desirable. Our culture usually values more highly the new, which is regarded as fresh, interesting, desirable. The new home, the new car, the new job – these represent advances. Advertisers describe products as "new and improved". This simple word-association suggests that an *Old* Testament (as well as the religion which it contains and its followers) is worn-out, outmoded, no longer functional, especially in contrast to the New (and improved) Testament.

Congregations need to be educated as to the effects of the adjectives "old" and "new" when applied to the parts of the

Bible and to Judaism ("old covenant") and to Christianity ("new covenant"). The simplest antidote is to speak simply of the Bible, since for the church sacred scriptures comprise the whole sixty-six books (and more if the Apocrypha is included). The order of service or worship bulletin, for instance, can refer to the reading(s) from the Bible or to the Scripture lesson(s) rather than to the reading from the Old Testament, the Gospel, etc. Given the pluralism and diversity of the Bible, there is little reason for preachers to use the all-inclusive terms "*The* Old Testament. . . . *The* New Testament". Generally, it will be better for preachers and those who lead worship to refer to the specific books of the Bible by name.

When one wishes to refer to the whole of the first thirty-nine or the last twenty-seven books, one can use phrases which neither denigrate nor elevate. For example, other ways of speaking of the first thirty-nine books include Hebrew Bible, sacred scriptures of Israel, the canonical Jewish literature, the holy writings of the Jews, the literature of Israel. The situation is somewhat more complicated in the case of the twenty-seven books which came from the hand of the early church, but one can still speak of them as the canonical literature from the early church or the canonical apostolic writings, or the early witnesses to Jesus.

Standing for the reading of the Gospel

Many congregations stand in order to honour the reading from one of the Gospels. Given the anti-Judaism present in many of the Gospel readings, the act of standing often has the effect of giving assent to anti-Judaism. Even when standing is intended to honour Jesus and God's work through Jesus, the standing itself implicitly approves the content of the reading. If the congregation is to stand, let it be for an affirmation of faith which is free of anti-Judaism.

Christianizing the Psalms

In some traditions and congregations, a trinitarian doxology is appended to the Psalm for the day or to other readings or liturgical acts drawn from the sacred literature of Israel. This addition causes the worshipper to read the Trinity into many passages and places where the Trinity is not really found, as if the simple monotheism of the text is insufficient. Such Christianizing violates both the literary integrity of the literature and impugns the theological integrity of all who do not confess the Trinity. It needs to be stopped. The service contains other places where the Trinity can be invoked without casting aspersion upon Judaism.

Selection of music

Much of the theology by which we live is the theology which we sing. Anti-Judaism is not as prevalent in the hymns of the church as it is in the literature from the early church. Indeed, many, many hymns affirm the wonderful love and work of God through Jesus without casting any aspersions upon Jews. Yet some hymns do contain anti-Judaism and should not be sung. Likewise, the music director or organist needs to be alerted to the dangers of anti-Judaism in anthems and other music in the service.

Christomonism in the liturgy

The church properly gives thanks to God for the life, death, resurrection and continuing presence of Jesus. Yet some churches so focus upon Jesus that God is all but forgotten. They are not only Christocentric but are Christomonistic. This can easily imply that it is possible to come to God only through Jesus. For example, some who lead worship pray almost exclusively to Jesus. Some preachers emphasize conversion to Jesus and faithfulness to Jesus without clarifying the ultimate theocentric goal of the Christian life. Yet one purpose of the doctrine of the Trinity is to preserve the ultimately theocentric character of

Christianity. Christian prayer, for instance, is directed to God; it is offered in the name of Jesus in order to confess that we come to know, love, worship and serve *God* through Jesus. Planners of worship need always to develop materials that have the glory of God as their goal. In this, Christians and Jews are one.

Language at the Lord's Table

The words spoken at the Lord's Table are the most important words in Christian worship. They express what we most fully think, feel and believe about God. With respect to anti-Judaism, the communion prayers are sometimes troubled by the same hermeneutic of prophecy and fulfilment that we saw in the lectionary. In the prayer which rehearses saving history, emphasis sometimes falls on the Israelites as murmurers and rebels whom the prophets comforted with the promise of the Messiah, with little recognition that God was acting for salvation in the history of Israel. Jesus is introduced into the prayer as "the answer" for Jews as well as for Christians.

This hermeneutic is neither appropriate nor necessary. The prayers in the newer worship books emphasize the continuity of God's saving work in the story of Israel and in the stories of Jesus and the church. Alongside the making of the covenant with Abraham and Sarah, the Exodus, the giving of the Law and the unfolding story of Israel, the act of God in Christ takes its place as a revelation of God.

In churches which do not use established service books and in which the communion prayers are prepared afresh for each new occasion, careful attention needs to be given to the appropriate use of themes from the life of Israel in them. This is especially true of churches like the Christian Church (Disciples of Christ), in which the communion prayers are prepared and led by the laity. Here, careful instruction is required.

Use of Jewish images and occasions

A simple way to help the congregation to develop a positive image of Judaism is for those who lead worship to employ images from the Jewish tradition in the liturgy. For example, in prayer, one might address God in speech that consciously evokes the memory of Israel. One might pray, "O living God, you opened the waters of the Red Sea and delivered your people from bondage in Egypt. . . ." Responsive readings and litanies are especially amenable to the use of words which come to us from the sacred scriptures of Judaism.

Those who lead worship can also explain the origin of those acts of Christian worship which have their roots in Judaism and of those Christian occasions and symbols which can adequately be understood only in the light of their Jewish background. The meaning of Pentecost, for example, is immensely deepened when we remember its meaning as a Jewish festival. And the attention of the congregation can easily be called to the occurrence and meaning of Jewish holy days. Passover, for instance, occurs near the time of Easter. A knowledge of Passover not only enhances the congregation's view of Judaism but enriches its appreciation of the Lord's Supper and of God's saving presence.

Avoiding stereotypes

Those who lead worship, especially preachers, need to speak of Jewish people as simply that – people who are Jews. Stereotypes are to be avoided. Examples of such stereotypes are references to "the typical Jewish mother", the "Jewish nose", or to the Jewish facility for making money. Some preachers have even spoken of "the Jew" as if all Jewish people could be compressed into a single way of thinking, feeling and acting.

Confession

The Christian community needs corporately to confess its own anti-Judaism, particularly the ways in which it has misrepresented Judaism, failed to witness to God's love for Jews and failed to act justly towards the Jewish community. Of course, care needs to be taken that contemporary Christians do not heap upon themselves responsibility and guilt for the long centuries of anti-Judaism and anti-Semitism. But, as in the case of all sin, we do need to assume responsibility for those inappropriate things which we have done. Honesty before God requires no less. The goal is not to feel bad but to identify those things for which we need to take the positive action of repentance. Freed by God's grace from bondage to anti-Judaism, we can embark on a new course marked by respect, love and justice.

Conclusion

The language we use goes a long way towards creating our perception of the world in which we live. Thus, if we speak of God as loving each and all, then we will come to see each one as beloved by God and as the object of our own love. And if we speak of God as commanding justice for each and all, then we will soon begin to shape all our language and behaviour in such a way as to be just. When viewed in this way, the words and actions of worship are critical to the elimination of anti-Judaism. Of course, the purpose of worship is never to promote any particular agenda. But when all of God's family – Jews and Gentiles alike – are recognized as recipients of God's love and justice, then the unbroken chorus of glory which rises to heaven's throne is itself a witness to God's undivided, unbroken love.

Bibliography

Abbott, Walter, M., SJ (ed.)
1966   *The Documents of Vatican II*, New York: The America Press

Ambrose
1956   Letters 40 and 41: The Synagogue at Callinicum, in *Early Latin Theology*, ed. and trans. S. L. Greenslade, London: SCM Press and Philadelphia: The Westminster Press

Augustine
1971   "The Lord's Prayer Explained to the Candidates for Baptism", in *Biblical Sermons to Savonarola*, ed. Clyde E. Fant Jr and William M. Pinson Jr, Waco, TX: Word Books
1975   "Sermon 156", in *Documents in Early Christian Thought*, ed. Maurice Wiles and Mark Santer, Cambridge: Cambridge University Press

Bailey, Lloyd
1977   "The Lectionary in Critical Perspective", *Interpretation* 31, 139–54

Barnabas
1947   "The Letter of Barnabas", trans. Francis K. Glimm, in *The Apostolic Fathers*, Vol. I of *The Fathers of the Church*, New York: CIMA Publishing Co., Inc.

Barrett, C. K.
1957   *The Epistle to the Romans*, Black's New Testament Commentaries and Harper's New Testament Commentaries, London: A & C Black and New York: Harper & Row

Barth, Markus
1959   *The Broken Wall*, London: Collins and Valley Forge: Judson Press
1974   *Ephesians 1–3*, Anchor Bible, Garden City: Doubleday & Company

Baum, Gregory
1979   "Catholic Dogma After Auschwitz", in *AntiSemitism and the*

Foundations of Christianity, ed. Alan T. Davies, New York: Paulist Press, 137–50

Betz, H. D.

1971   "The Cleansing of the Ten Lepers", *Journal of Biblical Literature*, 30, 314–28

1979   *Galatians*, Hermeneia, Philadelphia: Fortress Press

Blass, F. W. and A. Debrunner

1961   *A Greek Grammar of the New Testament and Other Early Christian Literature*, trans. R. W. Funk, Chicago: University of Chicago Press

Boadt, Lawrence, CSP, Helga Croner and Leon Klenicki (eds.)

1980   *Biblical Studies: Meeting Ground of Jews and Christians*, New York: Paulist Press

Bower, Peter (ed.)

1987   *Handbook for the Common Lectionary*, Philadelphia: Geneva Press

Brown, Raymond E. SS

1966   *The Gospel According to John*, Anchor Bible, Garden City: Doubleday & Company

Bultmann, Rudolf

1951   *Theology of the New Testament*, Vol. 1, trans. Kendrick Grobel, New York: Charles Scribner's Sons and London: SCM Press

1972   *The History of the Synoptic Tradition*, rev. ed., trans. John Marsh, Oxford: Basil Blackwell

Chrysostom, John

1975   "Homilies on I Corinthians 10. 16–17", in *Documents in Early Christian Thought*, ed. Maurice Wiles and Mark Santer, Cambridge: Cambridge University Press

1979   *Discourses Against Judaizing Christians*, trans. Paul W. Harkins, Washington, DC: The Catholic University of America Press

Cranfield, C. E. B.

1963   *The Gospel According to St. Mark*, Cambridge Greek Testament Commentary, Cambridge: Cambridge University Press

1979   *A Critical and Exegetical Commentary on the Epistle to the Romans*, International Critical Commentary, Edinburgh: T & T Clark and Greenwood, SC: The Attic Press

Cyril of Jerusalem

1975a   "Catechetical lecture 18.22–7", in *Documents in Early Christian Thought*, ed. Maurice Wiles and Mark Santer, Cambridge: Cambridge University Press

1975b "On the Mysteries 4 and 5", in *Documents in Early Christian Thought*, ed. Maurice Wiles and Mark Santer, Cambridge: Cambridge University Press

Dey, Lala Kalyan

1975 *The Intermediary World and Patterns of Perfection in Philo and Hebrews*, Society of Biblical Literature Dissertation Series, Missoula, Montana: Scholars Press

Dodd, C. H.

1944 *The Apostolic Preaching and Its Development*, London: Hodder & Stoughton and New York: Harper & Brothers

Efroymson, David P.

1976 *Tertullian's Anti-Judaism and its Role in his Theology*, Philadelphia: Temple University, PhD dissertation

1979 "The Patristic Connection", in *AntiSemitism and the Foundations of Christianity*, ed. Alan T. Davies, New York: Paulist Press, 98–117

Fant, Clyde E., Jr, and William M. Pinson, Jr (eds.)

1971a *Biblical Sermons To Savonarola. 20 Centuries of Great Preaching*, Volume One, Waco, TX: Word Books

1971b *Luther to Massilon. 20 Centuries of Great Preaching*, Volume Two, Waco, TX: Word Books

Farley, Edward and Hodgson, Peter C.

1985 "Scripture and Tradition", in *Christian Theology: An Introduction to Its Traditions and Tasks*, ed. Peter C. Hodgson and Robert H. King, Philadelphia: Fortress Press and London: SPCK, 61–87

Fisher, Eugene

1983 "The Impact of the Christian-Jewish Diaglogue on Biblical Studies", in *Christianity and Judaism: The Deepening Dialogue*, ed. Richard W. Rousseau, SJ, Scranton, PA: Ridge Row Press, 117–38

Fitzmyer, Joseph A., SJ

1985 *The Gospel According to Luke X–XXIV*, Anchor Bible, Garden City: Doubleday & Company

Gager, John G

1983 *The Origins of Anti-Semitism*, New York: Oxford University Press

Gaston, Lloyd

1979 "Paul and the Torah", in *AntiSemitism and the Foundations of Christianity*, ed. Alan T. Davies, New York: Paulist Press, 48–71

1980 "Abraham and the Righteousness of God", *Horizons in Biblical Theology* 2, 39–68

1982 "Angels and Gentiles in Early Judaism and in Paul (Galatians 3.19)", *Studies in Religion* 11, 65–75

1984 "Works of Law as a Subjective Genitive", *Studies in Religion* 13, 39–46

Glasser, Arthur F.

1986 "Truth As Revealed in Scripture", *Religion & Intellectual Life* III, 65–71

Glimm, Francis X., Joseph M.-F. Marque, SJ, and Gerald G. Walsh, SJ (trans.)

1947 *The Apostolic Fathers, The Fathers of the Church*, Volume One, New York: CIMA Publishing Co. Inc.

Granskou, David M.

1972 *Preaching on the Parables*, Philadelphia: Fortress Press

Grant, Robert M.

1986 *Gods and the One God*, Philadelphia: The Westminster Press

Greenslade, S. L. (trans. and ed.)

1956 *Early Latin Theology*, The Library of Christian Classics, Volume V, London: SCM Press and Philadelphia: The Westminster Press

Hare, Douglas R. A.

1967 *The Theme of Jewish Persecution of Christians in the Gospel According to St Matthew*, Cambridge: Cambridge University Press

1979 "The Rejection of the Jews in the Synoptic Gospels and Acts", in *AntiSemitism and the Foundations of Christianity*, ed. Alan T. Davies, New York: Paulist Press, 27–47

Harkins, Paul W.

1979 "Introduction", in *Discourses Against Judaizing Christians*, trans. Paul W. Harkins, Washington, DC: The Catholic University of America Press

Herford, R. Travers

1912 *Pharisaism: Its Aim and Method*, New York: G. P. Putnam's Sons

1924 *The Pharisees*, New York: The Macmillan Company

1928 *Judaism in the New Testament Period*, London: The Lindsey Press

Hippolytus

1975 "Apostolic Tradition 41–2", in *Documents in Early Christian Thought*, ed. Maurice Wiles and Mark Santer, Cambridge: Cambridge University Press

Irenaeus

1975   "Against the Heresies IV, 17.5–18.5", in *Documents in Early Christian Thought*, ed. Maurice Wiles and Mark Santer, Cambridge: Cambridge University Press

Jeremias, Joachim

1972   *The Parables of Jesus*, third rev. ed., trans. S. H. Hooke, London: SCM Press

Käsemann, Ernst

1980   The Epistle to the Romans, trans. Geoffrey Bromiley, Grand Rapids: Wm B. Eerdmans and London: SCM Press

Kesley, David

1985   "The Function of Scripture", in *Readings in Christian Theology*, ed. Peter C. Hodgson and Robert H. King, Philadelphia: Fortress Press and London: SPCK 50–9

Klein, Charlotte

1978   *Anti-Judaism in Christian Theology*, trans. Edward Quinn, Philadelphia: Fortress Press

Koenig, John

1979   *Jews and Christians in Dialogue*, Philadelphia: Westminster Press

Luther, Martin

1955–   *Luther's Works*, ed. Jaroslav Pelikan (56 vols), St Louis: Concordia Publishing House

1956   *Sermons on the Passion of Christ*, trans. E. Smid and J. T. Isensee, Rock Island, IL: Augustana Press

1961   "The Freedom of a Christian", in *Martin Luther: Selections From His Writings*, ed. John Dillenberger, Garden City, NY: Anchor Books

1971   "Whitsunday", in *Luther to Massilon*, ed. Clyde E. Fant, Jr and William M. Pinson, Jr, Waco, TX: Word Books

Martyn, J. Louis

1979   *History and Theology in the Fourth Gospel*, rev. ed., Nashville: Abingdon Press

1983   "A Law-Observant Mission to Gentiles: The Background to Galatians", *Michigan Quarterly Review*, 20, 221–36

Melito of Sardis

1979   *ON PASCHA and Fragments*, trans. and ed. Stuart George Hall, Oxford: The Clarendon Press

Moore, George Foot

1927   *Judaism* (3 volumes), Cambridge, Mass.: Harvard University Press.

Newbold, Robert T., Jr (ed.)

1977   *Black Preaching: Select Sermons in The Presbyterian Tradition*, Philadelphia: The Geneva Press

Ogden, Schubert M.

1961   *Christ Without Myth*, New York: Harper & Brothers and London: Collins

1976   "The Authority of Scripture for Theology", *Interpretation*, 30, 242–61

1982   *The Point of Christology*, San Francisco: Harper & Row and London: SCM Press

Origen

1971   "The First Homily", in *Biblical Sermons to Savonarola*, ed. Clyde E. Fant, Jr and William M. Pinson, Jr, Waco, TX: Word Books:

Parkes, James

1934   *The Conflict of the Church and the Synagogue*, New York: Hermon Press

1948   *Judaism and Christianity*, London: Gollancz and Chicago: The University of Chicago Press

1960   *The Foundations of Judaism and Christianity*, London: Vallentine, Mitchell and Chicago: Quadrangle Books

Pelikan, Jaroslav (ed.)

1967   *The Preaching of Chrysostom*, Philadelphia: Fortress Press

1985   *Jesus Through The Centuries: His Place in the History of Culture*, New Haven and London: Yale University Press

Perrin, Norman

1967   *Rediscovering the Teaching of Jesus*, London: SCM Press and New York: Harper & Row

Perrin, Norman and Dennis Duling

1982   *The New Testament: An Introduction*, rev. ed., New York: Harcourt, Brace, Jovanovich

Proclus

1975   "Sermon I", in *Documents in Early Christian Thought*, ed. Maurice Wiles and Mark Santer, Cambridge: Cambridge University Press

Pulpit Digest

1965   Edited by Ralph C. Raughley, Jr, Manhasset, NY: Pulpit
        Digest Publishing Company
1985   Edited by James W. Cox, Louisville, KY: Pulpit Digest

Quinley, Harold, and Charles Y. Glock

1979   *Anti-Semitism in America*, New York: The Free Press

Richardson, Peter and David Granskou (eds.)

1986   *Anti-Judaism in Early Christianity*, Waterloo: Wilfrid Laurier
        University Press

Rivkin, Ellis

1978   *A Hidden Revolution: The Pharisees' Search for the Kingdom Within*,
        Nashville: Abingdon Press
1984   *What Crucified Jesus?* Nashville: Abingdon Press and London:
        SCM Press

Ruether, Rosemary

1974   *Faith and Fratricide: The Theological Roots of Anti-Semitism*, New
        York: The Seabury Press
1983   *To Change The World: Christology and Cultural Criticism*, London:
        SCM Press and New York: The Crossroad Publishing
        Company

Sanders, E. P.

1977   *Paul and Palestinian Judaism*, London: SCM Press and Philadel-
        phia: Fortress Press
1983   *Paul, the Law and the Jewish People*, Philadelphia: Fortress Press
        and London: SCM Press
1985   *Jesus and Judaism*, London: SCM Press and Philadelphia:
        Fortress Press

Sanders, James A.

1983   "Canon and Calendar: An Alternative Lectionary Proposal",
        in *Social Themes of the Christian Year*, ed. Dieter Hessel, Philadel-
        phia: Geneva Press, 257–263
1984   *Canon and Community: A Guide to Canonical Criticism*, Philadel-
        phia: Fortress Press

Sandmel, Samuel

1978   *Anti-Semitism in the New Testament?*, Philadelphia: Fortress Press

Skudlarek, William

1981   *The Word in Worship*, Nashville: Abingdon Press

Sloyan, Gerard
1973   *Jesus on Trial*, Philadelphia: Fortress Press
1978   *Is Christ the End of the Law?*, Philadelphia: Westminster Press

Stambaugh, John E., and David L. Balch
1986   *The New Testament in Its Social Environment*, Philadelphia: The
       Westminster Press

Stark, Rodney, Bruce D. Foster, Charles Y. Glock and Harold E.
Quinley
1971   *Wayward Shepherds*, New York: Harper & Row

Stendahl, Krister
1976   *Paul Among Jews and Gentiles*, Philadelphia: Fortress Press and
       London: SCM Press

The New Pulpit Digest
1975   Edited by Charles L. Wallis, Jackson, MS: Walter Dell Davis
The Pulpit
1950
1951
1952   *A Periodical of Contemporary Preaching*, ed. Charles Clayton
       Morrison, Chicago: Christian Century Foundation

Tillich, Paul
1967   *Perspectives on Nineteenth and Twentieth Century Protestant Theology*,
       New York: Harper & Row and London: SCM Press

Townsend, John T.
1979   "The Gospel of John and the Jews: The Story of a Religious
       Divorce", in *AntiSemitism and the Foundations of Christianity*, ed.
       Alan T. Davies, New York: Paulist Press 72–97

Vermes, Geza
1974   *Jesus the Jew*, New York: The Macmillan Company, reissued
       Philadelphia: Fortress Press and London: SCM Press
1984   *Jesus and the World of Judaism*, Philadelphia: Fortress Press and
       London: SCM Press

Whitehead, Alfred North
1978   *Process and Reality* (ed. David Ray Griffin and Donald W.
       Sherburne), New York: The Free Press

Wiles, Maurice and Santer, Mark (eds.)
1975   *Documents In Early Christian Thought*, Cambridge: Cambridge
       University Press

Williams, D. Newell

1985   "The Devil's Use of Scripture", *CTS LINK* 20, 3

Williamson, Clark M.

1982   *Has God Rejected His People? Anti-Judaism in the Christian Church*,
        Nashville: Abingdon Press

Zwingli, Huldrych

1971   "On the Choice and Free Use of Foods', in *Luther to Massilon*,
        ed. Clyde E. Fant Jr and William M. Pinson, Jr, Waco, TX:
        Word Books

Index